Dr. Emeric Lebr

Doctor of Psychol

What I'd like to say to you...

If I could find the words, if I had more time, if...

Orient'Action® Publishing

Share your testimonials on Facebook Join the public group

WHAT I'D LIKE TO SAY TO YOU

ORIENT'ACTION® PUBLISHING:

Orient' Action® Publishing is a young publishing house specialising in personal and professional development books. Created in January 2014 by Emeric Lebreton, they allow you to discover the work carried out within Orient'Action® coaching firms. Every year, in France and abroad, thousands of people are supported in their professional and personal development. If you too want to make a change in your life and seek personal development, find us on **www.orientaction-groupe.com.**

ISBN: 9791096667482

Table of Contents

The stories told in this book...   5

Acknowledgements   7

Why did you write this book?   8

What I'd like to say to you...   11

Being lost in one's life   13

Losing a loved one   22

Seeing only your faults   33

Feeling like giving up   42

Suffering from pain   54

Seeking happiness   64

Being rejected by your loved ones   72

Going too fast   81

Being critical of our loved ones   91

Being angry   98

Refusing help   108

Facing a difficult problem   115

Losing self-confidence   125

"No..."   134

Seeing yourself grow old   141

Separating   151

Making an important decision   159

Suffering from bad luck   165

Adapting to change   172

Being in conflict   181

Goodbye   191

Bibliography   199

By the same author   200

One last story before you go...   201

The stories told in this book...

The stories told in this book were mostly dreamt up by unknown authors. They have been passed on through the ages, peddled by travelling storytellers and poets like seeds carried by the wind across the seas. They have been transformed, updated, modified, "polished like precious stones" by the talent of each storyteller. Today they can be found in films, on the internet, on social networks and of course in this book... They belong to humanity. They are fundamental teachings for being happy. They have inspired me greatly, and I have chosen to put them together and collect them to pass them on to you. Now it's your turn to tell them, to become a wise man or a poet in your turn...

Acknowledgements

I'd like to thank all the people I met on the path of life when writing this book. Each of these chapters is dedicated to one of them and it is therefore natural for me to dedicate this book to them, as they are partly its authors. I'd like to thank the philosophers, thinkers and sages from whom I have borrowed stories, remarks and quotations. This book is an opportunity for me to pay them heartfelt tribute. I'd also like to thank all the members of my Facebook community. I salute their generosity in making suggestions and positive comments. Finally, I'd like to warmly thank Élise Ducamp, publisher, who pushed me to write this book, as well as Anne-Sophie Thuard, bookseller, Véronique Germond, journalist, Marc-Olivier Goldmann, writer and proof-reader, Samira Qelaj, Béatrice Mathieu-Leloup and Marie Donzé, passionate readers, all members of the editorial committee for this book. When I look at the work completed, I realise that it is above all the work of a community and that my role was ultimately that of a humble messenger.

Why did you write this book?

On the path of life, I have come across many people. Around me are my loved ones and the people I love, and sensitive soul that I am, I can tell when these people are having problems or are not doing well. This affects me and makes me suffer with them. So I want to help them. I want them to be happy.

As I grew up and got older, I realized how difficult it was to help and talk about important issues with the people you love. You don't have the time, you don't have the words, you don't have the solutions, and they are not always ready to listen. They think we want to change them, dominate them, direct them.

Whether you are a parent, husband or wife, brother or sister, I'm sure that you've been faced with this situation at some point in your life. Someone close to you was suffering, making bad decisions, locking yourself into negative attitudes. You wanted to help them. You were sincere. But they refused to listen to you. They refused your advice.

I wrote this book to be a messenger, the messenger of those who want to help their fellow people, but cannot find the words, the time or the solutions to help them. Rather than trying to convince them or advise them yourself, I suggest giving them this book. When they are ready, they will read it and be enlightened.

**THIS BOOK IS A GIFT, TO YOURSELF
OR TO SOMEONE YOU LOVE.**

BEFORE YOU START

Name three animals that immediately come to mind

Write them in a corner of your mind.

What I'd like to say to you...

If I could find the words, if I had more time, if...

I love you and I have a deep affection for you. This means that every time you are not well, I'm not well, every time you encounter a problem, I encounter a problem, every time you are faced with a difficulty, I'm faced with a difficulty. Your situation touches me, and I sincerely want to see you happy and fulfilled in your life.

Whenever this happens, I'd like to help you get better, to find a solution, to solve a difficulty. Often I'm tempted to give you advice, but I don't dare. I'm afraid of making a mistake, of hurting you or of overstepping my role. I tell myself that maybe you just want to be listened to.

Sometimes I also lack time, energy or ideas. There are so many things going on in your life, things that are so complicated, that it is difficult for one man to pretend he knows how to solve them all. What to do when it comes to insoluble problems such as separation, sadness or the death of a loved one. How do you do it?

I have a deep respect for you, and you mean a lot in my life. Since I don't want to interfere in your life, to deal with things you wouldn't want me to do, I decided to give you this book. It was written by someone who is profoundly good, who has drawn inspiration from the greatest sages in the history of mankind to write it.

Don't feel obliged to read it right away. Wait patiently for that day when you think you could benefit from someone else's opinion. That day when you believe that others have experience or knowledge that can help you, then just take this book and read it. I hope you find it useful and inspiring.

I want you to be happy and fulfilled in your life. I want you to be free and to realise your dreams. This book probably sets out one or two ways to achieve this, a few stories to enlighten you, a few adages to make you think and help you. This book is another small brick in the construction of your own self.

See you soon in "real life" to talk and smile.

Being lost in one's life

WHEN I SAW YOU, YOU SEEMED TO BE LOOKING FOR
SOMETHING... YOU LOOKED LOST... ASKING YOURSELF
QUESTIONS AND PROCRASTINATING, YOU WERE
NO LONGER WILLING TO DARE...

THIS IS WHAT I'D HAVE LIKED TO TELL YOU...
IN YOU I SEE ALL THAT YOU CAN BRING TO OTHERS
AND TO THE WORLD...

...I'D PROBABLY HAVE STARTED BY TELLING YOU
ABOUT THE MEANING OF LIFE.

Every human being has a destiny. Someone who has stopped acting and is overwhelmed by questions is in fact in search of their own destiny. They are like a butterfly, in the state of a chrysalis, in transformation. They seek their destiny beyond the inheritance they have received, beyond what their parents or society wants to make of them. They are seeking it out beyond their fears, their hurdles and their heaviness. They are striving to make the star emerge from the depths of their heart, so they can launch it into the sky to guide their path.

You too have a fundamental mission to accomplish, which must give meaning to everything you do in your life. People who know their mission have confidence in themselves. They act. They hold it inside them, like a backbone that supports everything they do. And nothing can bend them or divert them from their goal. For they know why they were born and the reason for their time on this earth. They know the meaning of their lives.

• • •

In a faraway country, a woman was walking on a deserted beach at sunset. Gradually she saw the silhouette of a young girl on the horizon. As she approached she noticed that the girl kept bending over to pick up something and throw it back into the sea.

Tirelessly, she bent down, picked up something from the sand and threw it into the ocean. As she got closer, the woman noticed that the girl was actually picking up the starfish that the rising tide had washed up on the beach and throwing them back into the water one by one.

The woman was intrigued. She approached the girl and said, "Hello, can I ask you a question. I've been watching you for a while now and I was wondering what you are doing. "

"I cast the starfish back into the sea. It's low tide, you understand, and all these starfish have washed up on the beach. If I don't throw them back into the ocean, they will die." replied the girl.

The woman gave her a perplexed look before adding: "But there must be thousands of starfish on this immense beach. You won't be able to save them all. There are too many. And surely you realise that the same thing is happening on other beaches all over your country. Don't you see that you can't change the fate of these starfish".

The girl smiles. She bent down again and picked up another starfish. She put it back in the water and added: "That changes everything for this one!"

• • •

If you know the meaning of your life, you'll have great confidence in what you are doing. Nothing you do will ever seem in vain. You'll know what you have to do and why you choose to do it. And because you choose to do it, you'll live in harmony with yourself and the world around you. People who know the meaning of their lives are not afraid of difficulties or failures. Because they focus on their goal and each of their actions feels necessary and useful to them. They have faith in themselves.

• • •

*"In a pretty absurd universe, one thing is not absurd,
and that is what we can do for others."*

ANDRÉ MALRAUX

• • •

To find the meaning of your life, if you agree to do this exercise, you need to ask yourself four questions:

- The first question is: what are the values that guide my life?
- The second question is: what do I need to be happy?
- The third question is: what is my deepest personality?
- The fourth question is: what are my talents?

Find the answer to these four questions and then the meaning of your life will become clear to you. You'll know what country you should live in, what job you should do, who you should marry and what you should do each day to be happy and to make everyone around you happy too. Don't be too impatient-it often takes time to find the answer to each of these questions, as well as a great deal of self-knowledge.

. . .

"Nosce te ipsum*"*

SOCRATES

. . .

While writing this book, one day I discovered that my two guiding values are freedom and universalism. All my actions are made to make me freer every day while trying to change the world by making men and women better. From that day on, I knew who I was and what my destiny was. I felt a great happiness and stability inside me. And what about you? What is the value, the "will", that gives meaning to all your actions, every day?

Is it the will:

- to lead others like a prince?
- to live in the moment like an epicurean?
- to become the best in a sport, business or art like a champion?
- to change the world like a prophet?
- to perpetuate and defend traditions like a patriarch?
- to live with respect for moral values like an honest man?
- to take on new challenges like a conqueror?
- to live in security as a peaceful man?
- to do good around you by helping others like a wise man or a healer?
- to...?

It's up to you to find out...

. . .

---

* Know yourself.

"What is the value of men? What they seek. "

PERSIAN PROVERB

. . .

To find out what you need to be happy, try this exercise. Take a large vase and put it on a table. Next to the large vase, place five large stones, a bowl filled with small stones, a cup filled with sand, and a jug filled with water. The large stones represent what is most important to you in life, the small stones what satisfies your needs but is of secondary importance, the sand what can give you pleasure but is in fact unimportant, and the water what is superfluous.

Have fun filling this big vase. You'll find that if you want to fill it completely, you must first place the large stones, then the small stones, then the sand and finally the water. If you do the opposite, you won't be able to fill the vase.

- What are your big stones
  (what is essential for your happiness)?
- How small are your pebbles
  (what is useful for your happiness but not essential)?
- What is the sand in your life (what is superfluous)?
- What is the water (what is useless)?

By answering these four questions, you'll know what is really important to you and you'll make the right choices for your future life.

. . .

Now that you know what's really important to you, you need to know your inner self. Your inner self is who you are deep down inside. Your inner self is what you were before the world taught you to wear a mask. Your inner self is how you would think and behave, if you could do anything you wanted to do the way you wanted to do it. Then you would live in harmony with the world.

Knowing your inner self lets you know the country you should live in, the job you should do, the person you should marry and much more. You are then able to make the right choices; you no longer make choices to please others, to be liked or appreciated by others, or to avoid being criticised. You do things because they are good for you, because they give you pleasure and well-being and because they are consistent with your inner self.

• • •

"There are faces more beautiful than the mask that covers them."

JEAN-JACQUES ROUSSEAU

• • •

The last thing you need to discover are your gifts. Gifts are your talents, and everyone has a gift that is up to them to discover. Some are good at drawing, some at music, some at arts and crafts, some at organising, some at talking, and so forth, but a gift is often hidden behind a flaw. Gifts make you singular and unique. If you have a big flaw, that is probably your greatest quality. The question is what you can do with it to help others and make yourself useful.

Your gifts are there so you can create something that will be offered to others. In this way you'll only give back to other humans what nature has given you in abundance. A talkative person can talk for hours, a painter can draw for hours, an organiser can tidy for hours. When you use your gifts, you are never tired. You are inexhaustible. You take pleasure in what you do, and you get a lot of satisfaction in return.

• • •

*"The meaning of life is to find your gift.
The purpose of life is to share it."*

WILLIAM SHAKESPEARE

• • •

*"The meaning of life is to find your gift.
The purpose of life is to give it away."*

PABLO PICASSO

• • •

When you get to know yourself better, you'll know the meaning you want your life to have. You'll know your basic needs and your deep personality as well as your gifts, and then you'll know your place in the world. This place is what allows your inner being to live in harmony with your outer environment. This place is what allows you to achieve happiness and joy and at the same time make others happy and joyful. Finding this place is a great opportunity.

• • •

*"When I went to school,
They asked me what I want to be when I grew up.
I wrote down: Happy
They told me I didn't understand the assignment,
I replied that they didn't understand life."*

JOHN LENNON

• • •

This story took place a long time ago, when such large buildings were being built that they took multiple generations. For these constructions to succeed, a master architect was appointed to train the apprentices who would have the heavy task, once he died, of continuing the construction.

The master architect, judging his students' apprenticeship to be almost complete, sent them to the quarries to assess their skills and knowledge in stone cutting. He left them to work alone for several weeks before visiting them to assess their skills and talents.

And he approached one of them and said, "Tell me, my dear pupil, what are you doing?" The pupil raised his head and cast a dark glance in the direction of his teacher. He seemed very unhappy with his fate and the hard work he was required to do. "Master, you know very well that I cut stones hard all day long and that I'm a stonemason".

The teacher continued his inspection and saw a second pupil cutting the stone: "Tell me, my dear pupil, what are you doing?". The apprentice stood up and respectfully answered him: "Master, I work every day to carve the stone and to implement your teachings."

The master smiled ... encouraged the apprentice to continue his work and went on his way. Suddenly his gaze was drawn to a third apprentice. He seemed extremely focused on his task. He seemed to be totally absorbed by it. Approaching him, the master saw that the pupil, after cutting his stone, was polishing it with Love.

He asked him: "Tell me, my dear pupil, what are you doing?". The pupil stood up and raised the stone before him, and answered, his voice quivering with emotion: "Master, I'm building a cathedral."

If you are lost in your life, it is because you no longer know how to be useful. Ask yourself how you want to be useful to others. Ask yourself what kind of cathedral you are called upon to build. Then you'll see your true vocation appear. Beyond the trials, efforts and pleasures that are your daily life, you'll see the drawing of your life forming in the distance, like the one who looks at the clouds in the sky. Do not forget. Your actions and thoughts are the pencil with which you trace the shape of your destiny.

Losing a loved one

YESTERDAY, WHEN I WALKED THROUGH YOUR DOOR,
YOU THREW YOURSELF IN MY ARMS: YOU HAD JUST LOST
A LOVED ONE... YOU WERE FULL OF SADNESS
AND YOU WERE CRYING... I WAS OVERWHELMED
AND COULDN'T FIND THE WORDS...

THIS IS WHAT I'D HAVE LIKED TO TELL YOU...
IF I COULD HAVE DONE MORE THAN SHARE YOUR GRIEF...
IF MY THROAT HADN'T BEEN SO TIGHT THAT NO WORDS
COULD COME...

I WOULD PROBABLY HAVE STARTED BY TELLING YOU
THE STORY OF THIS MAN.

Once upon a time there lived a man and his family in a faraway country who lived peacefully from cultivating the land. This man's name was James. During the day, in the midst of the beautiful meadows that surrounded his house as far as the eye could see, Jacques cultivated the land. Every day, he gave thanks to the great river that bordered his house for bringing him water to water the cereals, vegetables and fruits that grew in his fields. James lived happily with his wife, daughter and two sons.

Every year, at the end of winter, the river flooded. It flooded part of the fields on its banks and the silt carried by the river water enriched the soil. One year, however, the flood was much stronger than usual. The water came up to Jacques' house, which was on the side of a hill. James brought his animals to the top of the hill for safety and refused to leave the house he had spent so many years building.

But the water continued to rise. It rained more and more every day. Although the water had invaded the ground floor of the house, Jacques refused to leave his house. Then the water rose to the ground floor, so Jacques then took refuge on the roof of his house, from where he contemplated his fields drowned by the water, which now formed a lake. His family was gone. Jacques was left alone with his strongest son on the roof of the house waiting for the river to disperse.

One evening, after a violent thunderstorm that had caused the river to rise again, a neighbour came with his boat to pick him up, just before his house was swallowed up. Jacques then moved to the top of a hill where he had kept a small barn, still waiting for the water to come down. He began trying to build dikes and pump the water out. But there was nothing to be done. It seemed that the river had changed its nature. In fact, a dam had given way upstream, and it was beyond repair.

All his friends advised him to give up farming and do something else. But Jacques refused because he knew that he had to be brave in life. "You did everything you could, you fought bravely. Now it's out of your hands," they told him. "Now you have to accept what has happened". When Jacques heard this became angry. He withdrew into himself. And when he was alone, he cried at losing this beautiful house and his life good.

Finally, after a few months, he came to his senses. He understood that there was no point in regretting what was lost. Instead of mourning what he had lost, he went back to work to make the most of what he had left, and with the strongest of his sons, he set about rebuilding another house. From time to time he still got angry and cried, but less and less often. In time he learned acceptance and could focus again on his future.

- The anger that haunted him abandoned him,
- The sadness dissipated,
- The joy returned.

He decided to go on a trip because he hadn't really rested for a long time. Along the way he met other men who lived by the river and who had also lost their homes. These men had decided to put traps in the river, which had become a lake, to catch fish. He loved this idea, and as soon as he returned home, he set off with the strongest of his sons to lay traps. The next day they ate delicious fish.

His life became that of a fisherman, and by the end of his life, he had become a respected and loved man, teaching many people how to set traps and catch fish. Many people in his country felt indebted to him because he had taught them how to feed themselves and save their families from the famine that was threatening them. On the day of his funeral, a stele was erected with the inscription: "*Here lies Jacques the fisherman*".

. . .

There are people who have experienced death, but who returned. Their heart stopped, their electroencephalogram was flat, the doctors were about to give up, convinced that it was all over. And then suddenly they took a deep breath. It was as if they had sunk to the very bottom of the sea, beyond what is possible, leaning on the bottom before coming to the surface. Life came rushing back into them. They were able to start again...

The people who have had this experience all tell the same story. They were walking through a tunnel, at the end of which was a beautiful light. Voices called them softly and encouraged them. They didn't feel any pain. They felt a sense of wellbeing. It was as if a burden had been lifted, making them light, relieved, calmed, serene to enter the light… And then they regained consciousness. They started to live again like before, yet differently…

• • •

"We have two lives, and the second begins when we realise we have only one."

CONFUCIUS

• • •

I'm telling you the story of these people who have experienced death to explain that this person, whom you love deeply and whom you have lost, did not suffer. When it was time to leave, they felt the same sensation as all those who made the final journey. This person reached the light at the end of the tunnel. They were fine, at peace. Everything was simple. They were was relieved and liberated, with no more difficulties, problems or pain. There was only peace.

• • •

There were two embryos in the uterus of a pregnant woman. The first was an optimist and the second a pessimist. The pessimist spoke up and said, "How can anyone believe in life after childbirth?"

The optimist replied: "I'm sure there is life after childbirth. Our time in our mother's womb has no other meaning than to prepare us for life after childbirth. Childbirth is not the end, but a new birth."

The pessimist replied: "What you say is false. There can be no life after childbirth. What form would such a life take? Anyway, no one has ever come back from childbirth to tell of what happens afterwards."

The optimist added: "I'm sure the world that awaits us after childbirth is a world full of light. We will be able to see with our eyes, smell with our nose, eat with our mouth and even run with our legs and..."

The pessimist objected: "What you are saying is ridiculous. Mere inventions. How could we run? And eat with our mouths? What use would it be when we have this umbilical cord that feeds us and attaches us to our world."

The optimist added with hope: "It must be possible! Life afterwards is very different. We are going to discover extraordinary things. We will discover extraordinary abilities and a wonderful world."

The pessimist immediately contradicts him: "You have to face the facts. With childbirth, life is over. This is our destiny as embryos. And afterwards there is only nothingness. After birth, we will disappear. "

The optimist nodded: "I agree with you on at least one point: we don't know what comes next. I'm sure that after our birth we will meet our mother and she will take care of us."

The pessimist sneered: "A mother? Do you believe in a mother? But who is she? What does she look like? And what exactly does she do for us? Your imagination is running riot. You should be a little more reasonable with your crazy ideas."

The optimist adds: "Our mother is all around us. She is that wall that protects us, that cord that nourishes us, that warmth that warms us, that water in which our body floats... We live in her and through her. Without her we would not exist."

The pessimist sneered again: "It's the height of madness! I've never seen any evidence of any mother. This mother you are talking about is a figment of your imagination to reassure you because you are afraid of being born."

The optimist added in a clear voice: "Sometimes, when a beneficial calm appears, I can hear her singing. It's like a vibration that surrounds us. It caresses our world. So I feel her presence and I can't wait to meet her."

• • •

"No one yet knows whether everything lives only to die or dies only to be reborn."

MARGUERITE YOURCENAR

• • •

For Hindus, at the moment of death, the spirit separates from the body. While some find the door to liberation, most souls seek a new body, and the spirit is reincarnated. Through this process, beings live through experiences that allow them to learn and evolve spiritually. Once they reach enlightenment they cease being reborn. According to the life one has lived, according to one's karma, one is reincarnated as a beast, a stone, a tree or a human being. A new life then begins.

For the Egyptians, death was merely a special moment in life that was expected and prepared for throughout life, so they prepared for their departure from an early age. They had to build and decorate their tombs, prepare the objects they would take with them so that they would lack for nothing, make donations and provide the necessary money for the priests. Their whole life on earth was merely a preparation for life after death, the life of the immortal soul. Were they right to believe this?

Among the Amerindians, it was believed that men and women had two souls. One that was attached to the body and the other that could leave the body, during sleep, illness or in a trance. When a man or woman died, their soul immediately joined the spirit world. The spirits then remained in contact with the living and could also attach themselves to the bodies of the living. Legend has it that this was the fate of the famous singer Jim Morrison.

In the summer of 1949, Steve and Clara Morrison took their children on holiday. On the road, they came across an overturned truck, with injured Indians lying on the road. Five-year-old Jimmy stares out the window and starts sobbing: an old Indian doctor, lying on the side of the road, stares at Jimmy, smiles and dies. Years later, having become a rock star, Jimmy would refer to it as the "most important moment of his life". For Jim Morrison, that day, the soul of the dead shaman entered his body.

• • •

*"Those who live in the hearts they leave
behind are not dead."*

NATIVE AMERICAN PROVERB

• • •

I'm sure that the person you love, the one who has now departed, has been reincarnated. Maybe she has become a beautiful flower that you'll see one day by the side of the road. Take the time to stop and marvel at her beauty. Maybe she has become one of those birds that sing at your window in the early morning. Take the time to listen to her sing. Or maybe she's that tree that gives you shade in the summer heat. Take the time to breathe its smell and fall asleep at its feet.

Pay attention because this person is there, I'm sure, somewhere around you. If you feel a sincere love for her, it means that you are connected, and I'm sure that you'll cross her path. You'll feel her presence and then you'll know that she's there. You'll know it and your heart will be soothed because she has become something good. These are signs of the presence of those you have loved, who have disappeared, but who continue to live with the living in another form.

• • •

"If you love a flower that lives on a star,
It is sweet to look at the sky at night."

THE LITTLE PRINCE, ST EXUPÉRY

• • •

There are three things that can prevent us from handling the loss of a loved one. The first is regret. We may regret not having spent enough time with the person we have lost, not having told them something important to them, not having helped them enough. They left too soon, we didn't have the time to say, to do, to think... Now that they've disappeared, we think it's impossible. So it's very hard to forget.

Close your eyes. Think very hard about the loved one you've lost. Remember their face, their smell, the sound of their voice, their presence... And speak. Say what you would have liked to say. Do what you would have liked to do with her. Kiss them and hold them in your arms. Live what you would have liked to live with this person. Don't be afraid to enter into a relationship with the invisible. Have confidence and you'll see your regrets fade away, making you whole again.

. . .

The second thing that can prevent us from processing the loss of a loved one is guilt. Did we do enough to avoid the worst, to hold onto them, to protect them? Guilt is anger directed at oneself. To recover from guilt, you have to recover from anger. To recover from anger, you have to accept that you are not responsible for what happened. We are powerless to change the course of events and to change the choices that have been made.

. . .

The third thing that can prevent us from processing a loss is a sense of injustice. When we are children, school, our parents and society teach us that the world is just. Adults tell us: if you behave well, you'll be rewarded. But if you do wrong, you'll be punished. So we believe that this law also applies to nature and life. We believe the innocent have the right to be happy and that they will be spared death, sickness and sorrow.

This is not true. Nature knows nothing of justice. It is ignorant of the laws of Men. In life, the innocent suffer as much punishment as the guilty, so to process the loss of a loved one, to mourn, one must first renounce the idea of justice. You must first look at the world as it is. And then you need to forgive it for not being more just, for not respecting the order you'd like it to. Yu must forgive it so you can continue to live in it.

. . .

The time has come. You must look away. The living are calling you. They need your attention. They need your support, your courage, your energy... Go and take care of them for a time and be patient. The unacceptable end will soon dissipate into your own end. Life passes quickly and you'll soon be reunited with your loved ones – there's need to be in a hurry that's for sure. Be safe in the knowledge that after life, you'll see them again. They haven't said goodbye, just au revoir.

• • •

The night is never complete.
There is always, as I say,
Since I say so,
At the end of sorrow
One open window, one illuminated window

There's always a dream waiting to happen,
Desire to satisfy, Hunger to satisfy,
A generous heart,
An outstretched hand, an open hand,
Attentive eyes,
A life, a life to be shared.
The night is never complete

PAUL ÉLUARD

• • •

One day, when I was in pain, a friend told me that he didn't get sad when he lost people. "How?" I asked him in amazement. He replied that the departed continued to live in his heart. To see them again, to listen to them and talk to them, all he had to do was close his eyes and feel their presence. Then, as if by magic, they would appear. He would spend a little time with them conversing or just saying nothing, making the most of their presence.

Maybe you too can close your eyes and think about that person you've lost and whom you love. Maybe you can look for their presence in your heart. Maybe you can still feel the Love that you have for them and they for you. Listen, feel, look. With your eyes closed, concentrated on your breathing, go deep inside yourself and then you'll find this being that you thought had disappeared and that in fact continues to live in your heart and all around you.

• • •

"May I be given the strength to endure what cannot be changed and the courage to change what can be changed but also the wisdom to distinguish one from the other."

MARCUS – AURELIUS

• • •

You know, you have a right to be sad. You have the right to want to be alone and to cry. What I'd like to say to you is that I think a lot of you. If you need anything, call me. I will come and visit you. We can talk, take our minds off things, have a coffee or even do nothing. We'll spend some time together and we'll laugh and cry. When the burden is too heavy to bear, you need to get together with other people to carry it. I'll help you bear your burdens. What I'd like you to know is that I'm there for you.

Seeing only your faults

WHEN WE LAST MET, YOU TOLD ME A LOT ABOUT
YOUR FAULTS... I HAD THE FEELING THAT YOU HAD LOST
CONFIDENCE IN YOURSELF...

WHEN I GOT HOME, I BLAMED MYSELF FOR FAILING TO
FIND THE WORDS THAT COULD HAVE COMFORTED YOU.

THIS IS WHAT I'D HAVE LIKED TO TELL YOU...
TO MAKE YOU SEE ALL THE WONDERFUL AND UNIQUE
THINGS INSIDE OF YOU...

...I WOULD PROBABLY HAVE STARTED BY TELLING YOU
THIS INSPIRING STORY.

In India, a water carrier held a wooden rod on his shoulders with two large jars hanging from each side. One of them was cracked and lost half of its precious cargo with each voyage. The other, in perfect condition, kept all its spring water until it reached the master's house. So the perfect jar would swagger, every day managing to fulfil its function without fail. The faulty jar, on the other hand, was depressed to accomplish only half of its work.

After two years, the damaged jar spoke to the water carrier while he was filling it at the spring. "I feel guilty; please forgive me," it said. "Why do you need to apologise?" asked the astonished water bearer. Surprised, the jar reacted: "During these two years, it is my fault that, despite all your efforts, at the end of each journey you only deliver half of my water to our master. You don't get full recognition for your efforts."

Touched by this, the water carrier replied to this confession: "Well, today as we return to the master's house, I want you to pay more attention and look at the vegetation along the path." As they climbed, the damaged jar, filled with wonder, saw beautiful flowers along the way. But at the end of the journey, it still felt as bad as ever because once again it had lost half of its water.

When he arrived at his master's house, the water carrier said to the jar: "So, did you realise that there are only beautiful flowers on YOUR side, and hardly any on the side of the perfect jar? I always knew you were losing water and I took advantage of it. On your side of the path I planted flower seeds because I knew that they would be watered every day. For two years I was able, thanks to you, to pick flowers that decorated the master's table. Without you I could never have found such beautiful and graceful flowers.

. . .

In San Francisco, there is a street on a hill called *Lombard Street*. This street is the only one in the whole city that is curved. In American cities, the streets are straight and rectangular, while in Europe, it's the other way around, the streets are crooked. This curvy street is a strange street. It's flawed! But as a result, it attracts tourists from all over the United States, who are surprised and amazed by this weirdness. This street is an attraction and one day I'd like to walk down it with you.

. . .

One fine spring morning, a farmer and his son were taking their donkey to the market to sell it. The father and his son walked, and the donkey followed. No sooner had they taken a few steps than they met a group of girls walking in the opposite direction.

– Look at them! exclaimed one of the girls, pointing at the farmer, – How stupid they are! They're walking on foot when they could be riding their donkey!

Hearing this, the old man quietly told his son to get on the back of the donkey and then they continued on their way to the market...

They passed a group of men sitting on the side of the road and the farmer heard one of the men say:

– Young people have lost all respect for their old parents these days. That lazy boy should give his father a rest!

So the son leapt down, and his father took his place...

Soon they came across a group of women with their children.

– Look at this cruel man! they exclaimed.

– He walks so fast that the poor boy can barely keep up!

The farmer then stopped and lifted the boy up and put him behind him.

They continued on their way and had almost reached the market when a trader stopped them.

– Is this your donkey? he asked.

– Yes! replied the farmer.

– Well, I'm shocked at the way you treat him, added the shopkeeper.

– Two people on the back of a donkey is too much! You'll kill him – you should carry him instead!

Following this advice, the farmer and his son got off the donkey, tied its legs and carried it on a wooden beam. But the donkey refused to be carried in this way and while struggling, it broke the rope that was holding its legs and fell into a river near the road and drowned. The farmer could do nothing, so they returned home empty-handed.

. . .

When I look at you, I see many qualities. There are many wonderful things about you. If I appreciate your presence, if I like to see and hear you and feel you with me, it's because I think you are a beautiful person. I see so many positive things that I believe you deserve to have a good life, to meet beautiful people and to be happy. I wanted to tell you this because usually I can't find the words and I'm too scared to tell you what I really think.

When I look at you, I see a lot of potential, a lot of possibilities. The future lies before you, and I tell myself that with all your knowledge, you could do many great things. I know you have dreams and I'm convinced you can make them come true because you have the qualities and the inner strength to do so. It's just a matter of attention and intention. Just look in the right place and you'll see that you can do it. Dare to desire the best for yourself and it will happen.

. . .

I once heard about a child who was said to be retarded. He spent hours lost in his thoughts and had fallen behind in his reading and writing. His classmates made fun of him, his teachers didn't know what to do, his parents were worried sick. The child's name was Albert Einstein, a distinguished researcher and Nobel Prize winner in physics who was behind many technological advances that are still used today for the good of humanity. The idiot turned out to be a genius!

. . .

Perhaps you suffer from your "physical imperfections". Physical appearance is a hugely important part of yourself, and sociology and history are particularly enlightening on this subject. Did you know that in Thailand, Korea or Taiwan, men with prominent noses are considered very attractive? Did you know that in some countries women freely display their hair, while in others their curves are admired? In each culture, flaws and qualities are assessed according to their own criteria.

• • •

If you agree, I think it can be said that a characteristic only becomes a quality or a defect depending on the context. Maybe if you only see imperfections in yourself, you are not in the right context. Where you are, what you are is not naturally valued. But you just have to change context, go to the right place, be with the right people. Try to imagine where or with whom all your faults could magically turn into qualities!

• • •

Many people think that you have to be perfect to be loved. This shows a lack of understanding of psychology. There have been many scientific studies that show the opposite. In fact, people love people who have both qualities and faults. You need both. It's like a balance. Too many faults can be repulsive. Too many qualities can frighten people off. Perfection is scary! A good mix of the two is what is needed. That's what makes you human.

Think back to your best holiday. I'm sure that the ones you remember best are precisely those that offered you the best moments of friendship, discovery and adventure, but with a few difficult moments. These moments are the imperfections that really make the experience. They are the ones that, by contrast, strike your memory like a coin. Holidays, people, places... you remember what is both so perfect and so imperfect.

• • •

Let me tell you the story of the "K". Stefano is a young boy. Early in his life he finds himself the victim of what he believes to be a curse, chased by a sea monster that looks like a giant shark. This giant shark is called "the K". All his life, Stefano naturally tries to get away from this monster, staying as far from the shore as possible. But as he gets older it's as if he's called by the sea. He then becomes a sailor and travels the world on his boat. In his boat, he flees "the K", like the worst of curses.

As he is about to die of old age, tired of running away, Stefano finally chooses to meet his destiny and face "the K". He discovers a fish which is also old and tired and had actually meant no harm to him. It was pursuing him because he'd been tasked with sending him a message. He had been entrusted with handing him a magic pearl with the ability to ensure his success, wealth and happiness throughout his life. Stefano then realised that he had refused his destiny until the twilight of his life[*].

• • •

Aren't what you see as flaws just "the K", that big, terrifying shark. Aren't your faults actually signs? Shouldn't you be using them to succeed and blossom elsewhere? Shouldn't someone who is disorganised accept that he is an artist? Shouldn't someone who is talkative accept that he is in fact a great communicator? And the grumbler that his anger is destined to make him change the world by fighting injustice?

• • •

---

* This text is freely inspired by the book: The "*K*" (1966).

In truth, your faults are the signs of your uniqueness. You should clearly not try to conform to what is expected of you, but rather try to be what you really are. Your faults are like the stars in the sky that guide the captain of a ship. They are what must guide you, for it is in them that a hidden part of your being's potential lies. Even the worst flaws can be turned into something extraordinary. Affirm them. Never be afraid of criticism.

• • •

- Disorder creates works of art,
- The grumbler changes the world,
- Shy people listen,
- Lazy people improve processes,
- The madman innovates,
- The hoarder preserves,
- Big people help little people and vice versa

Every human being has a place in the world.

• • •

- If someone wanted a brush with perfection, they'd have to pass you by!
- If perfection does not exist on earth, then what planet do you live on?
- Perfection exists on earth; you are the living proof!
- No matter how hard you try. You can never be anything but awesome!
- Your face is perfectly symmetrical, like a sketch by Leonardo da Vinci.
- You bring light to my life.
- With you, there's never a dull moment.
- You are the sugar in my corn flakes!
- You have more charm than Brad Pitt and Angelina Jolie put together.

...

What goes "TIC" 999 and "TOC" once?

Listen to your 999 legs that go "TIC" instead of listening to the one that goes "TOC".

...

We need revolt against those who want to put us in boxes. Those who criticize you are wrong – they're just people whose minds are too closed to accept difference and humanity. Their minds are like those little square offices found in the endless corridors of big administrations in the former USSR. The same offices, the same size, all grey and uninteresting. This is what their perfect spirit promises us, a world without shine, without colour, without magic.

...

Of course, some defects can still make you suffer. In this case, you probably just need to have some compassion for yourself. Speak to yourself as you would to a friend who is confiding his pain in you. Talk to yourself as someone who wishes you well, with kindness and empathy. Your words should be like caresses that soothe your tormented heart, like a mother's warm breath on her child's skinned knee. Give as much compassion to yourself as you do to the flesh of your flesh.

...

See your defects as an opportunity for progress, as an invitation to self-development. Criticism can be positive – when you are pricked, you are forced to react. And the person who pricks you, whatever his intention, good or bad, has actually done you a favour. He has caused you to question yourself, to go in search of a new version of yourself. This quest set you in motion, and by setting you in motion, it made you more alive. So why not thank all the critics for giving you the push you needed?

• • •

"Whoever consciously recognises his limits is the closest to perfection."

GOETHE

• • •

What I'd have liked to say to you, in fact, is simply that I love you. I love you and therefore I don't care what your qualities and faults are, because I love you as you are. I don't want you to change. You can change if you want to, but I just want you to be good, to be happy and fulfilled, because whenever you are happy, I'm happy too. Whenever you laugh, I laugh too. Every time I see you glowing and smiling, I glow and smile too. You inspire me.

I myself am full of flaws and imperfections. I'm not always attentive, sufficiently present, funny or understanding. I'm not as handsome as I could be, as friendly and funny as I should be. Sometimes I even behave like a real idiot. I'm an imperfection in your life. I'm a flaw. But if you'd accept me anyway, then I'd be happy. You could teach me how to improve myself and I'd be grateful.

Feeling like giving up

WHEN I SAW YOU, YOU WERE TIRED...
YOU WERE DEALING WTH MANY PROBLEMS
AND YOU FELT LIKE YOU COULDN'T COPE...
YOU FELT LIKE GIVING UP...

THIS IS WHAT I'D HAVE LIKED TO TELL YOU...
TO AWAKEN YOUR FAITH, THE FIRE AND THE STRENGTH
THAT LIVE INSIDE YOU...

...I WOULD PROBABLY HAVE STARTED BY TELLING YOU
THIS STORY.

Once upon a time there were two frogs that had fallen into a bowl of cream. The two frogs couldn't swim in the cream, which was too thick, and they couldn't get out because the edges of the bowl were too high.

After a few minutes, they were exhausted from struggling to escape. They were finding it increasingly difficult to get to the surface and catch their breath. They were going to drown. One of them said:

"I've got no more strength. We'll never manage to get out. I'm going to die. I don't see why I should continue to struggle, since we are condemned to die in this bowl anyway."

Having said this, it stopped struggling and disappeared, engulfed by the thick white liquid.

The other frog, more obstinate, tells itself: "It's impossible! There is no way out. Yet, although death is near, I will fight until my last breath. I refuse to die like this without doing anything."

It continued to thrash around in the same place, without moving forward, for hours and hours. And then suddenly, by dint of beating its thighs, shaking and struggling, the cream turned into butter.

Surprised, the frog leapt up and skated to the edge of the bowl, from where it happily croaked its way home.

• • •

When you are struggling to solve a difficulty or overcome an obstacle, your actions may seem futile. But in fact, they are not. What you fail to see is that every action you take is like a seed you plant. Some of these actions will yield important results in a short time. You just can't see it because you're too focused on the problem to be solved. It's because the seeds haven't yet had time to germinate, to grow and give beautiful fruit.

• • •

A young captain had decided to make a long journey. He wanted to go to America because he had heard that one could make their fortune there. Everybody said: America is the country where everything is possible! So he sold everything he owned, and with this money he bought a ship and hired a crew. It was June, the perfect time for long crossings, so one beautiful sunny afternoon, he set sail, certain he would reach the American coast in less than three weeks.

The first week went as he had imagined. The boat was fast, the crew efficient and motivated, the weather good. With a strong wind behind it, the boat set sail all the way to America but on the seventh day, the weather changed. It was about ten miles from the Caribbean when the sky suddenly became as black as night. The wind picked up and began to blow in violent gusts. Heavy rain began to fall on the bridge. A bolt of lightning split the sky.

In a few minutes, the wind became so strong that it tore the sails like paper. Lightning shattered the mast, and the waves became so high that they came over the rail and engulfed all the sailors in a muffled scream. After a few hours fighting bravely against the forces of nature, all that was left was the young captain clinging to the helm of the boat, which was drifting in the storm, tossed about like a tiny piece of wood.

It was then that a gigantic wave hit the deck, breaking the ship in two. It was swallowed up in a second. When the young captain came to, he found himself alone in the middle of the angry ocean, still hanging on to the helm of the floating ship and riding it on the crest of the waves. The storm went on for a long time: several hours or days, the young captain couldn't tell. He clung with all the energy of despair to the piece of wood that kept him on the surface and kept him alive. And then the storm disappeared as quickly as suddenly as it had arrived. The sun was shining high in the blue sky and the sea was like oil.

The young captain looked around him. He was alone in the middle of a huge saltwater desert infested with sharks, and at that moment he knew he was lost. No ship passed by this route because he had preferred to take a little-known route to save time. He had nothing to drink and nothing to eat. His mind was in turmoil. At that moment he knew he was condemned to death, so he asked himself this question: should I continue to swim, to resist fatigue, hunger and thirst, or should I resign myself to my fate and let myself die?

While he was pondering his fate, he looked around again. There was only water, except...He squinted his eyes. He seemed to see a dark spot in the distance. He rubbed his eyes, thinking he was dreaming. But no, there was something in the distance that seemed to float on the water. A boat, a reef, an island or a mirage...This place was tens of kilometres away, an impossible distance for a man in his tired state but the young captain didn't give it a second thought. He felt his strength returning. He thought of America, of that powerful dream that had made him give up a quiet life to go on an adventure and discover the world. He grabbed a floating bar and started to swim towards the mysterious black spot. He knew he had little chance of making it, but he had a chance! He had to make it.

He was moving very slowly. In the day the sun burned his face, at night he was paralysed with cold. Everywhere hurt but the pain didn't matter to him, because now he had a goal. He was gripped by thirst and hunger, which made him suffer horribly. Fortunately, after the second day it rained. He was able to drink a little from a container he had collected from the shipwreck.

He swam for three days and three nights after which he reached the beach of an island where, exhausted, he lay down on the sand. He could hardly move, but he was alive. A native man was passing and went to warn the other members of his village, who hurried to come and see the stranger. They gave him food and drink and treated his injuries, and when he finally recovered from this terrible ordeal, he built himself a raft and resumed his journey. A few days later, he arrived in New York Bay where he made his fortune and fulfilled his dreams. Now nothing could stop him.

• • •

To regain strength, you must remember your purpose. You have a purpose in your life. You want health, happiness, fame, fortune, freedom... or all of the above. It doesn't really matter what your goal is. Just close your eyes. Concentrate. Visualise your goal. Visualise it very specifically. If you want to get rich, imagine yourself sitting on a pile of gold, if you want to find a job, imagine yourself going to your new job, if you want to find love, imagine yourself with the man or woman of your life walking hand in hand.

You need to visualise your goal and place it clearly in the centre of your mind. Once it is in the centre of your mind, you must illuminate it with all the light of your soul and heart. Now, if you think about your goal, nothing can distract you from it. Your mind and body are like a questing head. All you need to do is live normally because you'll act without being aware of it, so your dream will come true. You'll always be moving in the right direction.

And if you want, you can even make your own visualisation board: cut out a large piece of cardboard and have fun sticking pictures, drawings, quotes... to it, which correspond to your goals. Place this board somewhere you can admire it every day. And every day, you'll remember your goals and the means of achieving them... This painting will give you strength and perseverance to hold on to your goals. It will give you the strength to succeed.

• • •

You're tired …
We're not tired
Olé

You're tired
We're not tired

The girls are tired
We're not tired

The guys are tired
We're not tired

POPULAR SONG

• • •

When you want to change your inner state, there is a technique called NLP (Neuro-Linguistic Programming) which consists of communicating with one's inner being to change one's inner state. NLP teaches us that we are masters of what we think and feel, so if you feel like it, you can change your inner states as easily as you would change your clothes. You can go from sadness to joy, from despair to fighting spirit.

If you're tired, if you feel like giving up and want to find that flame that usually burns in you, then remember back to a day when you were full of courage. Remember a time in your life when your determination was unquenched. That day, remember, nothing could stop you. You looked like you had eaten a lion! Remember how old you were. Remember who you were. Remember what you saw, what you heard, what you felt inside.

If you concentrate enough, if you search and find this memory then suddenly you'll feel the strength of this memory imbuing your present. You'll feel the courage, the strength and the determination come back to you. And you'll fight once again because nothing can beat you down. You're invincible! Concentrate, remember, let the emotions of the past invade you again. Let the past come back into your present and transform you. You feel the strength coming back to you. For you are a warrior of light.

. . .

"What is a Warrior of Light?
-You know him. He is the one who is able to understand
the miracle of life, to fight to the end for what he believes in,
and-then-to hear the bells that the sea rings in its depths."

"The Warrior of Light believes.
Because he believes in miracles, miracles begin to happen."

PAULO COELHO, MANUAL OF THE WARRIOR OF LIGHT

. . .

"Excuse me... I'm a lost kiss... Can I rest on your cheek?"

ANONYMOUS

. . .

If you no longer have the strength, it may be that your goal is too difficult to achieve alone. Ask your friends, family, colleagues, strangers for help... Human beings are gifted with empathy and are naturally inclined to help others so just ask them. Just be humble, accept that you don't have the strength to do it on your own. You'll see, once you dare to ask, you'll feel relieved. Never forget this motto that can help you in difficult times: *one for all and all for one!*

· · ·

*"When two forces are joined together,
their effectiveness is double."*

ISAAC NEWTON

· · ·

"What does not kill me makes me stronger."

FRÉDÉRIC NIETZSCHE

· · ·

*"Most of the important things in the world have been
accomplished by people who kept trying when there seems
to be no hope."*

DALE CARNEGIE

· · ·

Amazon shamans tell us that every man and woman has a totem animal which lives inside us and gives us the energy and strength to live and survive. When a person falls ill or encounters a problem, the shaman organises a ceremony where he puts the soul of the person in contact with his totem animal: the horse, the leopard, the snake, etc. The totem animal is what gives us the energy and the strength to live and survive. By reconnecting with their totem animal, the person recovers their strength and courage.

So what's your totem animal...? Is it the tiger that possesses agility, the eagle that can see from far away, the horse that can travel long distances, the camel that can go several weeks without eating or drinking a drop of water...? Look inside yourself for your totem animal – it will be the animal you naturally resemble. If you think about it, it will appear to you in a second. Let your intuition guide you and help you reconnect with the deep forces that lie within you.

• • •

Risin' up, back on the street
Took my time, took my chances
Went the distance, now I'm back on my feet
Just a man and his will to survive

So many times, it happens too fast
You trade your passion for glory
Don't lose your grip on the dreams of the past
You must fight just to keep them alive

EXCERPT FROM THE SONG "THE EYE OF THE TIGER..."
SONG FROM THE MOVIE ROCKY

• • •

Three men had a dream of climbing the highest peak in the world. So they went to the Himalayas at the foot of Mount *Everest*. They were perfectly prepared, extremely well trained, equipped with the most modern equipment and accompanied by the best Sherpas. The three men were excited to make their dream come true and began to climb with a feeling of elation towards the snow-white summit that was clearly visible in the blue sky.

The first days went very well. The weather was splendid, and they were still at a relatively low altitude. When you climb *Everest,* the difficulties increase as you get closer to the summit, as oxygen becomes scarce, the temperature drops, and the wind gets stronger. At the end of the seventh day, when they reached an altitude camp only a thousand metres from the summit, they felt, despite their fatigue, that they were going to make their dream come true. Their hearts were filled with hope and courage.

The next day, at dawn, they began the ascent. Everything was going well but around noon the north wind picked up. At this altitude, the wind was icy, and the higher they climbed the more difficult things became. One of the men, the more cautious one, proposed going back down, which was accepted by the second man, who was less cautious by nature, but who predicted a strong storm. The first man, who wanted to make it that very day, refused, and continued on his way in the wind and snow.

The two men went back down to the camp and waited for the end of the terrible storm. Two days later, the good weather returned so they resumed their ascent. It was their last chance to succeed because the season for climbing *Everest* was ending the next day, which marked the start of the rainy season began which made the climb impossible. They started their ascent normally, but again around noon, the north wind picked up and a thick fog fell on the mountain.

The third man, the more cautious one, suggested to the second man that they go back down. But this time the second man, seeing his dream slipping away, declined, so he continued on his way in the fog while the third man went back down to the valley. He was sad because he knew that he wouldn't be able to attempt the ascent for a long time. Because it was a long and expensive journey, and he didn't have enough money.

So he returned to his country. He worked hard and saved, and five long years passed before he returned to the slopes of the Himalayas. He had not given up on his dream. The ascent was difficult because he was older and had less strength than before, but with the help of his Sherpa, he reached the point where he had stopped five years earlier. The next day a storm was forecast, and he was afraid that he would have to come down again, but when he rose at dawn it was very sunny.

He climbed for a hundred metres before he came upon his first corpse. It was one of the men who had accompanied him on his first ascent and had frozen to death. He continued to climb and came upon the body of the second man who had also frozen to death. The sight made him really reflect on life, and when he reached the summit and finally realised his dream, he said to himself: if the difficulties become too great, learn to be patient. If the difficulties become even greater, learn to give up.

But never give up on your dream, because one day it will come true!

A true story told by a mountaineering friend
who climbed Everest in 2016.

• • •

"We don't know how to give up anything.
We only know how to exchange one thing for another."

SIGMUND FREUD

• • •

When you're tired, when you lose your courage, come to me and I'll help you as best I can. I could also help you decide whether you should persevere, wait or give up on a project that is too complicated or too difficult. But as I'm convinced that you must achieve your dreams, I'll also encourage you to continue to hope and to act to achieve them. I'm so eager to see your face light up with joy when you achieve what you want to that I'm ready to do everything it takes to help you.

• • •

"You must always aim for the moon, because even
if you fail, you'll land in the stars."

OSCAR WILDE

• • •

Top 3 most tenacious people in the world:
1. The Emperor
2. His wife
3. The Little Prince

• • •

On Monday morning, the emperor,
his wife and the little prince came to my house
to shake my hand, but since I had left, the little prince said,
since that we will return on Tuesday… Tuesday morning,
the emperor, his wife and the little prince…

SONG FOR CHILDREN

Suffering from pain

THE LAST TIME WE SAW EACH OTHER, YOU WERE
IN TERRIBLE PAIN. THE PAIN WAS CONSTANT, TO THE
EXTENT THAT YOU FELT IT WOULD ALWAYS BE THERE

THIS IS WHAT I'D HAVE LIKED TO TELL YOU...
TO MAKE YOU FEEL BETTER... TO MAKE YOU FEEL GOOD
AND HEALTHY...

...I WOULD PROBABLY HAVE STARTED BY TELLING YOU
THIS SALTY LITTLE TALE.

Once upon a time a grandmother, who was tired of hearing her grandson complaining incessantly, asked him to fetch some salt. When he came back from the supermarket, the grandmother asked her grandson to mix a large spoonful of salt in a glass of water and drink it.

"What does it taste like?" she asked.
"It's salty" replied her grandson, grimacing.
The grandmother laughed heartily and asked her grandson to pour the same amount of salt into the nearby lake. "Now drink water from the lake" she said.
The grandson did what he was told and took a sip of the pure water from the mountain lake. His grandmother asked him again: "What does it taste like?"
"The water's fresh and it tastes like snow" he replied with a big smile. "Did you taste the salt?" asked his grandmother.

"No," he replied.

The grandmother sat down next to her grandson and explained to him in gently:

"The pain we feel is represented by the salt. The amount of pain remains exactly the same. However, the amount you feel depends on the "container" in which you place your pain. So when you are in pain, the only thing you can do is to broaden your perception of things. Stop being a glass. Become a lake."

• • •

Congenital insensitivity to pain is a rare genetic disorder which often has very serious consequences. This disease results in the loss of the sense of pain in all its forms and on all parts of the body. The person retains their sense of touch but is unable to distinguish what hurts from what does not. For example, they can distinguish between hot and cold but cannot tell when they are burning. This obviously poses major problems.

This disease appears in early childhood and results in multiple traumas because the child does not realise that they have been hurt, being able to burn, bump, and scratch themselves without feeling any pain. This disease can therefore be very dangerous because children can be seriously injured without realizing it. It usually results in premature death, not because of the disease itself but because of the resulting traumas.

• • •

Pain is useful in life. It allows you to detect dangers and it keeps you from hurting yourself and your body. Pain is what stops you from burning yourself, jumping from a height, running too fast, hitting something too hard, etc. Pain is what keeps you from burning yourself. It is not a problem in itself – it helps you to make the right decisions and to act correctly. But sometimes this useful mechanism can go wrong. In this case, pain occurs when no solution can be found. You are in pain but there seems to be no cure.

• • •

Once upon a time a young boy looked at himself in the mirror. He discovered a small white spot. At first he didn't pay much attention to it, but the next day the little white spot caught his attention– it seemed to have grown. He wasn't sure, but it looked like it...He was worried because he was going to a party with other boys his age the following Saturday night, a party attended by a girl he had fallen in love with.

When he looked at himself in the mirror the next day, this time he was certain the spot had grown. He felt like it was the only thing anyone could see in the middle of his face, so he decided to do something about it. He took a lotion that his mother used to cleanse the skin and began to rub the spot vigorously to try to get rid of it. When he was finished, the pimple, far from having disappeared, was bright red. He had rubbed so much that it had irritated his skin.

It was a rather difficult day. Whenever he had a free moment, he would go to the toilet and look at himself in the mirror. The spot wouldn't go away, and neither would the rash. Around noon he cracked and tried to pierce the pimple with the tips of his nails. He pressed hard on it hoping to squeeze it, but it wouldn't pop. It became even whiter on the inside and redder all around. It seemed to be swelling by the moment.

When he got home in the evening, he borrowed a sewing kit from his parents, took a needle and pierced it in the centre. This time, victory! The spot was pierced, and a whitish liquid leaked out. He went to bed happy, but the next morning, when he stood in front of the mirror, the situation had worsened. Not only was the spot white again, but the dirty needle had infected it. It had spread and the skin around it was inflamed. All you could see in the middle of his face was the spot.

The spot was getting worse. The boy now had an infection. It was a wound that refused to heal. He visited several doctors who gave him creams, ointments, antibiotic drugs. Some of them tried to pierce it in turn. But none of these things helped. The situation got even worse, to the point that the boy thought he was going to die from a facial infection. Now he was afraid that he would be completely disfigured and become terribly ugly.

One day, at the end of his tether, he went back to the doctor. The doctor had gone on holiday and he had to see a substitute who was young and inexperienced but was actually an excellent doctor. When he saw the spot, he simply said, "stop touching it, think of something else and you'll see, it will heal". The young boy stopped touching it and oddly enough after seven days it was completely healed. He was the one who had caused and maintained the infection* by touching the spot.

• • •

Pain is not a reality. It is a perception which is composed of three dimensions:

- Fear of pain: I'm afraid of being in pain.
- The experience of pain: I'm in pain.
- The memory of the pain: I remember when I was in pain.

_____

* I must tell you the truth. This boy is me at the age of 23.

If you stop focusing on pain, then you'll remove two of these components: fear of pain and the memory of pain. In this way you can get real relief and sometimes even healing. If, on the other hand, you focus only on the pain, then that's all you'll be able to think about. You'll become pain and your life will become impossible. Hypnosis can help you, if you wish, to broaden your perception and reduce fear and the memory of pain. Try this technique for relief.

• • •

Doctor, I really don't understand what's happening to me.
When I touch my heart, it really hurts. When I touch
my liver it also really hurts, and when I touch my stomach
it hurts even more. I'm afraid I've got cancer.
Could you give me your diagnosis?
– Yes, of course, in my opinion, you have a broken finger!

• • •

When it hurts, do this exercise. Start by focusing on your pain. Try to feel it. You need to focus all your attention on your pain to understand every facet of it. This will help you gain a better understanding of your pain. Once you have done this, compare it to something, like an object, an animal, a phenomenon, etc. Try to symbolise it with something you know that could represent your pain.

Maybe your pain is as sharp as the tip of a needle, or it burns like fire, or it's like hammer blows raining down on your bones, or like pliers that crush... Find something that can represent your pain, that can symbolise it. Once you have found something that can represent your pain, you'll be able to change the perception of your pain by modifying the thing that represents it, by playing with your mind.

- Dull the needle,
- Throw water on the fire to quench it,
- Turns the iron hammer into a foam hammer,
- And the steel clip in a piece of rubber,
- Imagine the object of pain moving away, becoming blurred and then disappearing,
- Etc.

By doing this exercise, you'll discover that you have the power to change the perception of your pain and the power to vary the intensity of this perception. Maybe you won't be able to make it disappear completely at first, or maybe you will… The important thing is that you discover this power within yourself that allows you to change sensations and perceptions, to reduce pain and increase joy through the simple exercise of the will and the mind.

• • •

Pain is a messenger, if you are suffering from it somewhere, listen to its message:

- If your eyes hurt, close your eyes,
- If your foot hurts, stop walking,
- If you are suffering from liver pain, eat fruit and vegetables,
- If you have a headache, stay in a quiet place, away from the noise of the world and the light,
- If your back hurts, put down the burden that is weighing you down.

Pain is very often the result of abuse, excess or repeated bad behaviour. Before the pain came, there were signs that you didn't know how to listen to. Learn to listen to your body and your pain will go away over time. Listen to what you feel. Don't strain certain organs unnecessarily. Treat your body with gentleness and respect and it will give back to you with pleasant and sensual feelings. Health and its wonderful sensations will be your reward.

. . .

"Be wise, O my sorrow, and be still!"

CHARLES BAUDELAIRE.

. . .

Food is the cause of a great deal of suffering in your body. If you are suffering, try changing the quantity and quality of what you eat. Fruits and vegetables are like medicines – they can help you cure many illnesses, but on the other hand, some foods, because they are too fatty, full of sugar or have been processed too much, can make you sick and turn out to be real poisons. Try to change your diet.

For example, we know that milk is an indigestible substance that causes a host of problems such as joint pain or rheumatism. Milk consumption also causes you to gain weight, which is a burden on your back, knees and hips. Try to stop drinking milk and eating dairy products. Stop for a few days and see if this leads to an improvement. There are many other foods to keep an eye on that can increase your pain. Be alert.

. . .

"Let food be your first medicine."

HIPPOCRATES

. . .

In addition to physical pain, there is also the psychological pain of anger born out of a sense of injustice. What have I done to deserve to suffer like this? It's true, pain is absurd and unjust, but all the same it is there. What's the point of being angry? What's the point of being angry at the whole world and at yourself for suffering? It just adds to the pain and robs you of the energy to deal with it. All you can do is accept your pain and confront it.

• • •

"Here below, sorrow to sorrow follows one another;
day follows day, and sorrow follows sorrow. "

ALPHONSE DE LAMARTINE

• • •

Remember, people have two souls. The first soul lives in the body. It is attached to it. It is the breath that animates it. It is like a vibration. When you are fully present in yourself, this is the soul you use, and it is through it that you perceive the world. The second soul lives outside the body and all around it. It is free like a bird; it can fly to other worlds. You use your second soul when you are dreaming, thinking or meditating.

When you are in pain, you may be tempted to use your second soul because it allows you to escape pain. You may be tempted to take medication or use alcohol because it nourishes your second soul and helps you escape your pain. But remember – only your first soul can help you heal. It's by grounding yourself in your body, it's by confronting your pain that you awaken the miraculous forces of life within you. For your first soul invites your body to heal.

• • •

"Mens sana in corpore sano"*

JUVENAL

. . .

Physical pain can be caused by psychological pain. Work, marriage and family are all possible causes of your pain or discomfort.

- If there are conflicts, they should be resolved,
- If there are tensions, they should be eased,
- If you feel you don't fit in, then move.

For your body to be healthy and suffer less pain, you need to live in a place that suits you with people who are right for you. Don't add to your pain by making the wrong choices.

. . .

*"Man's body is a vessel on which the soul embarks
to cross a stormy sea."*

AXEL OXENSTIERN

. . .

*"I took the two FFs out of the verb to suFFer,
now I'm fine!" (a play on words in French,
"SouFFrir" (suffer) turns to "Sourir" (to smile)*

ANONYMOUS

. . .

---

* A healthy mind in a healthy body.

If you're in pain, seek my advice and I'll give you some ideas on how to try to ease it. There must be a path to wellness. There is always a way to find relief – hypnosis, acupuncture, yoga, meditation, fasting, physical activity and traditional medicine, etc., can all help. And remember one key thing: there is a medicine that your loved ones can give you to help you recover and soothe your pain; it's called Love.

Seeking happiness

WHAT A JOY IT WAS TO SEE YOU HAPPY AND FULFILLED
YESTERDAY!

THIS IS WHAT I'D HAVE LIKED TO TELL YOU...
IF I HAD DARED... TO ENSURE YOU'RE ALWAYS HAPPY...
SO THAT YOUR SMILES CONTINUE TO LIGHT UP MY LIFE...

...I WOULD PROBABLY HAVE STARTED BY TELLING YOU
THIS STORY.

A mother and her youngest daughter were walking in the mountains. Suddenly the girl slipped on a stone and fell. She hurt herself and shouted: "Ai!!!!"
To her astonishment, she heard a voice in the mountain repeating: "Ai! Ouch! Ouch!"
Curious, she asked: "Who are you?"
And the voice in the mountain answered her, "Who are you?"
Annoyed by this answer (the girl was a strong character and hated people repeating everything she said like a parrot), she shouted: "You're a coward!" And the voice in the mountain shouted: "Coward, coward, coward!"
The girl looked at her mother in disbelief: "What's going on Mummy?"
The mother replied with a smile: "Listen carefully now my darling". And she shouted very loudly to the mountain: "I think you're wonderful".

The voice in the mountain repeated three times: "I think you're wonderful".

She shouted again: "You're the most beautiful and intelligent of all little girls".

The voice repeated three times: "You're the most beautiful and intelligent of all little girls".

"I love you; I adore you". The voice repeated three times: "I love you, I adore you".

The young girl still didn't understand what was happening, except that her mother's words had filled her heart with joy.

Then her mother explained it to her.

"This phenomenon is called an echo. In some places, when you speak, your voice reverberates and comes back to you, as if multiplied. It's the same thing that happens in life – everything you do or say has an echo. If you're happy and you share your happiness and joy, then your happiness and joy spreads and eventually comes back to you. If you want more happiness in the world, start by filling your heart with happiness and your joy will spread to everyone you meet and then come back to you as an echo."

• • •

One day, a woman coming out of her house came across three old men standing on her doormat. All three had long white beards and they looked as old as the world. As she did not know them, the woman said to them: "I don't think I know you, what are you doing standing on my doormat?" The three old men replied in unison, "We're hungry, we don't suppose you have anything for us to eat?"

The woman looked at them with surprise and then answered kindly: "Yes, of course!" This woman was generous and the three old men had aroused her curiosity. "Come in, make yourself at home."

When hearing these words, the three old men stiffened and added.

"But the three of us never enter a house at the same time."

"And why?" asked the woman, amazed.

These three old men were decidedly strange.

One of the old men explained to her:

"My friend's name is Wealth, he is Success and I am Love. So you have to decide which of the three of us you want to let into your house first."

The woman was perplexed, so she went inside to her husband. She presented the situation to him and asked his advice.

"What a boon," he said. Wealth, Success and Love are knocking at our door at the same time. Hurry up and let Wealth in before he changes his mind."

His wife listened and then thought.

"Dear husband, why don't we invite Success in instead," she asked.

Their daughter, who was in a nearby room, overheard their conversation. She too had an opinion.

"Shouldn't we invite Love in first? That way, our house would be filled with Love and we would be happy!"

Husband and wife trusted their daughter who was a very wise child. So the wife returned to the doorstep and invited Love in.

"Love, it has been decided, you are our guest!"

Love entered the house. The other two old men followed him and entered in turn.

The woman was astonished. She asked Wealth and Success: "I only invited Love in. Why are you also coming in? I thought the three of you never went into the same house."

The old men answered him in unison: "If you had invited Wealth or Success in, the other two would have stayed outside, but since you invited Love in, wherever he goes, we go with him. You know, Madam, wherever there is Love, there is also Wealth and Success!!!!"

. . .

Two hundred people were attending a seminar. Suddenly, the speaker stopped talking and gave each person a balloon. Then he invited each participant to write their name on the balloon in a large, fun text. All the balloons were collected in a nearby room and the speaker then asked each participant to go into the room one by one to find their balloon (the one with their first name on it!) and all within five minutes. All the participants rushed into the room and started looking for their balloons. They pushed, shoved and ran around in a cloud of dust and a deafening noise. The deadline had passed, and no one had been able to find their balloon.

Then the speaker said: "I now suggest that each participant takes a balloon at random and offers it to the person whose name is written on it." Within a few minutes, everyone had their balloon back. The speaker then said: "The exercise you have just done is a reflection of what is happening in our lives. Everyone is seeking happiness, not knowing where to find it, whereas real happiness lies in the happiness of others. If you help people you know to find happiness, you'll find happiness too. You must think as much about the interests of others as you do about your own interests. And in this way you can create harmony in your relationships with others."

• • •

If you're lucky enough to be happy, share your joy and happiness with the people you meet. Smile and laugh and make others smile and laugh too. Share – don't be stingy. Some people will resent you for being happy when they are unhappy. Don't let them bring you down – be an example, because just as an ice cube melts in the sun, their faces will eventually light up with a smile. Your joy will vanquish their pain.

• • •

"Happiness is only true when it is shared."

JON KRAKAUER, INTO THE WILD

• • •

If you are happy when reading these lines, you need to make sure that this state lasts forever. You may be happy because of the circumstances: maybe it's summer and the heat and the sunlight are filling you with joy. It's great to know how to enjoy the miracle of summer so make the most of it to make a promise to yourself to stay happy even when circumstances have changed, even when the sky is grey, it's rainy and windy and freezing cold. That is your challenge!

• • •

Being happy every day is not as simple as it seems. Most people who are suffering or encounter insoluble problems in their lives resent happy people. Joy, smiles and laughter irritate them. The Happy Man symbolises the injustice they feel they are suffering. We need to have compassion for these people and welcome their sometimes-harsh criticisms and comments without deviating from one's credo of living happily whatever happens.

• • •

Paradoxically, happy people encounter more problems and difficulties than other people. They are spared nothing. If you smile and look happy, people will assume you're strong, and if you're strong you'll be tested. This will happen mainly in your work, but also in your friendships or family life. In general, people demand much more of happy people than unhappy people, while suffering and unhappiness are excellent excuses to be left in peace.

• • •

Veils on the girls
Boats on the Nile
I'm in your life
I'm in your arms
Alexandra Alexandria
Alexandria where love dances with the night
I have more appetite
Than a Barracuda
I'll drink the whole Nile if you don't hold me back.
I'll drink the whole Nile if you don't hold me back.

Alexandria
Alexandra
Alexandria where love dances in the sheets
Tonight I have a fever and you are freezing to death.
The sirens of the port of Alexandria
Still singing the same wowo melody
The light of the Alexandria lighthouse

ALEXANDRIA, ALEXANDRA
CLAUDE FRANÇOIS, 1972

• • •

That's why it's not easy to choose to be happy, because there are many advantages to being unhappy. It's true that you suffer, but there are also many benefits. People listen and feel sorry for unhappy people. They show understanding and forgiveness towards them. They even let them do things that people are not usually allowed to do, such as being obnoxious or unpleasant, getting angry and saying bad things. Being happy is much harder.

• • •

"To live is to wake up at night in anticipation of the day
to come, is to marvel that the daily miracle
is happening for us once again, is to have insomnia from joy."

PAUL-EMILE VICTOR

• • •

Happy people have joy as their goal. Happiness is for them like a target, a stone to which their soul is anchored. They cling to joy like a mould to its rock. Storms pass, the wind blows, the sun blazes and they are always there. And as they cling to joy, they turn everything that happens to them into opportunities, occasions, pretexts to improve their situation even more. Happiness attracts further happiness and luck.

• • •

Happiness is made of energy,
Of perseverance and faith:
If you want to attract it to you,
Tirelessly, work and pray.

"Help yourself the sky will help you"
Whoever is distrustful of fate
Less than someone else will fix it.

HENRI-FRÉDÉRIC AMIEL

• • •

Happy like Ulysses, has made a beautiful journey, punctuated by many trials, separations, betrayals and misery, but also encounters, beautiful stories of love and friendship. This is life, a beautiful journey that one must relish, the only one you take, like a painter who only had the right to paint a single work. He would paint it in colours, and it would undoubtedly be the most beautiful. Travel, you the one I love and who I see is happy, enjoy the wind and the calm sea; the weather is beautiful today.

• • •

This is the story of a strawberry that goes horse riding:
clip clop, clip clop..

• • •

I want you to be happy every day of your life. You must be honest – at times things will be hard, so it's up to you to make a choice, to be happy no matter what happens. If you can choose to be happy no matter what happens, then you'll be able to overcome all of life's trials and tribulations without complaining and letting yourself go. You'll move forward with your head held high, proud and serene. You'll become an example to follow and you'll brighten the lives of everyone you meet.

Being rejected by your loved ones

RECENTLY, IN THAT PLACE WHERE WE OFTEN MEET,
YOU CONFIDED TO ME THAT YOU HAVE BEEN REJECTED
BY PEOPLE YOU LOVE..

THIS IS WHAT I'D HAVE LIKED TO TELL YOU...
IF I COULD HAVE SHOWN YOU WHAT YOUR
TRUE VALUE IS...

...I WOULD PROBABLY HAVE STARTED BY TELLING YOU
THIS STORY ABOUT A GOAT.

Once upon a time there was a village. In this village, men and women sinned and acted immorally on a regular basis. The fact that everyone was sinning caused many problems in the village. There were frequent conflicts between the inhabitants and resentment was beginning to build up between them. The first had betrayed someone, the second had cheated, the third had stolen, the fourth had hurt someone... etc.

The village chief, fearing that these conflicts might lead to violence, went to seek the advice of a wise man who lived in the mountains. The wise man replied: "Take the ugliest and smelliest goat in your herd. Once you have chosen it, ask each villager to write their grievances against the other villagers on a piece of bark. When this is done, hang the bark around the goat's neck and then beat the goat with a stick through the village.

When he has passed through the village and you have hit him hard, scare him so badly that he runs into the desert at the hottest hour of the day. Make sure that all the villagers see you do this and understand that the goat will die in the thirsty, sun-burned desert. In this way, all the sins of the villagers will be forgiven and forgotten, and normal life can resume." As soon as the chief returned, he organised the great ceremony. The goat was exiled and died, and peace returned to the village.

Thus the rite of the scapegoat was born.

• • •

Human psychology is based on the rejection of difference. Difference excites curiosity less often than it repels it. Whether the difference is physical like the colour of the skin, social like religion, or psychological like an opinion, difference always provokes resentment, i.e. anger, which manifests itself through mockery and bullying, then physical violence and can even go as far as murder. This is how groups protect their traditions.

Why does difference cause anger?

Someone different seems to be a critic. They don't necessarily want to criticise, but that's how they're perceived. They're actions are seen as questioning or even challenging the values, behaviour or beliefs of the group. This questioning creates disorder and ultimately leads to uncertainty, and therefore anxiety. Someone who is different causes anxiety, and to reduce this anxiety, people try to bring them into line. And if they don't accept it, we attack them.

• • •

"Truths that are different in appearance are like countless leaves that look different and are on the same tree."

GANDHI

• • •

If you're rejected, it is because you've become different, different from other members of your family, friends, colleagues etc., and this difference fuels resentment towards you.

- Maybe you have done better than the others?
- Maybe you have made different life choices?
- Maybe you dress or wear your hair differently?
- No doubt you have learned to assert yourself through these choices?

All this makes you a problem. You look like a critic and in return you provoke violence, contempt and rejection.

This is not necessarily expressed directly. They don't say: "I don't love you, or you annoy me because the way you think and act is different to mine". It's more insidious, but you feel it. It is expressed in the way they look at you, the way the address you, the way they react to your presence; you can feel it in the vibes that people give off in your presence… Then there are the little jokes and remarks, seemingly innocuous but hurtful. Because your heart knows what's going on. It isn't fooled. Your heart sees everything.

• • •

"Humour is sometimes a disguised form of violence."

ANONYMOUS

• • •

Oh, if you only knew how I feel this tear in your heart, when those you love push you away. Yes, you have chosen to live your life, but do you deserve to be judged and denied the friendship and affection of a father, mother, brother or sister, cousin or friend? Love is the fierce desire to see a person grow and be happy. And you are being offered quite the opposite. People want you to stop being you. They want you to give up your own path to follow another that you never chose.

• • •

What can you do? Do you have to give up being you? Do you have to become what they expect to be, to be loved in return? Or should you assert your difference and live your life? I'm going to tell you something difficult, but something that reflects reality. If you are rejected, you have only two choices: to conform to the expectations of those close to you, to "fit into the mould to be accepted" or to "cultivate your difference" and in this case you must consider meeting new people who will love you for who you are.

• • •

"From what I know of history, I see that humanity cannot do without scapegoats. I believe that they have always been an indispensable institution."

ARTHUR KOESTLER

• • •

When you are rejected by those you love, start by having compassion for yourself, the victim. Accept this rejection as you accept the rain or the sun. Then you can have compassion for those who reject you because most of them are just ignorant. They are not aware of what they are doing, what they are saying, where this feeling comes from. They might not even be aware that they are hurting you. They don't realise their criticisms affect you.

• • •

The great Buddha once came to speak in a village and all the men, women and children had gathered to listen to him. But soon a very violent man arrived who found the Buddha exasperating. He began to insult the great Buddha, before leaving, red with anger. As he left the village, the man felt his anger subside and gradually a deep sense of shame came over him. How could he have behaved like that in public?

He decided to retrace his steps and ask the Buddha for forgiveness. The Buddha was still speaking, and he waited until the end of his speech to prostrate himself at his feet and ask his forgiveness. Buddha, full of compassion, asked him to get up, explaining that there was nothing to forgive. Surprised, the man reminded him of the insults he had made in public against him. He could not have forgotten the words he had spoken in anger.

"What do you do if someone gives you something for no reason that you don't need or want?" asked the Buddha.
"Well, I just don't take it," replied the man.
"What does the person who tried to give it to you then do?" asked the Buddha.
"Well, they keep their object," replied the man.
"This is probably why you are suffering from the insults you uttered. As for me, rest assured, I was not burdened by your insults. Nobody agreed to accept the violence that you wanted to spread."

• • •

You can't decide what people think of you. You can't control their love and you must let them be free of what they think and do. If what you do pleases them, arouses their interest or admiration, be happy. If they don't like what you do, if they are indifferent or disdainful, be happy too. Enjoy doing what you like and being yourself. Remember the story of the donkey, the farmer and his son. There will always be someone in this world to criticise you.

• • •

"Having meditated on gentleness and compassion, I have forgotten the difference between myself and others."

MILAREPA

• • •

Life is about change. You must learn to get out of the way of those who are inconsiderate towards you. Just move away from them, as you move away from the sun on hot days. If a person wishes you ill, then you must get away from them. Otherwise, in the same way that a careless person who stays too long in the sun burns his skin, you'll suffer from despair and distress. You need to surround yourself with people who accept you and love you as you are.

• • •

"The human mind treats a new idea in the same way that its body would treat a strange protein; it rejects it."

PETER MEDAWAR

• • •

For your part, be careful not to reject anyone. Every man and every woman can find it hard to accept certain differences. Even the most tolerant of men and the most tolerant of women are sometimes intolerant. Learn to be humble and to be careful and discerning about your opinions and behaviour. That way you'll make sure you never reject anyone and never put others through what has hurt you. Be tolerant and welcome difference as an opportunity.

• • •

"An honest man is a mixed man."

MONTAIGNE

Never underestimate the difficulty. Anyone who has lived with strangers for a long time knows how difficult it is to be a mixed man. If you are aware of the effort you have to make to reach out to others, to understand them and to try to build bridges with them, then you'll be all the more willing to do so. You can then become a ferryman, one who is able to put different people in touch with each other. In this way you'll help create and maintain peace in the world, because misunderstanding is often the cause of conflict.

• • •

"Be the change you want to see in the world."

GANDHI

• • •

Maybe you were rejected as a child. A few years ago I remember reading the story of Carrot Top, a little boy who was hated by his family because he had red hair, which he couldn't do anything about. Being rejected as a child is one of the most terrible things that can happen to a human being, because children cannot defend themselves against rejection. They are not free to seek out people who are able to accept them as they are and love them for what they are.

If you were rejected as a child, you might still have a deep wound in your heart. If this wound has not yet healed, then it might reopen whenever you find yourself cast aside. If this is the case, you need to heal this wound, but how? How do you fill the gaping hole you fall into when others push you aside and criticise you? How can you fill that dark bottomless pit?

There is an energy capable of this miracle. This energy is called Love. It is not the Love of others, no – we cannot expect such a miracle from others. It is the Love that emanates from your inner being. The problem people who were rejected as children face is not that they were insufficiently loved. Their problem is that no one taught them to love, let alone to love themselves. They lack the instruction manual for Love.

If you want, I can try to teach you to love you. Just close your eyes. Start by feeling your body. Feel every part of it inside and outside. Think of yourself as the parent of your inner child, a loving and caring parent who gives you all the care you need. Take care of your body. Take care of your mind. Protect. Heal. Nourish. Warm. Caress. Love. Practice until you feel the vibration of Love, the vibration that breathes life into your being.

• • •

*"As I began to love myself, I freed myself of anything
that is no good for my health – food, people,
things, situations, and everything that drew me down
and away from myself...At first I called this attitude
a healthy egoism. Today I know it is love of oneself."*

CHARLIE CHAPLIN

• • •

If one day you are rejected by those you love, or painful memories are making you sad, know that you can come to me. I have decided to love you no matter what happens and no matter what you become. I'm your friend and I will remain your friend because I have made this choice and I'm committed to it. If the day comes when you reject people in turn, then I give myself permission to tell you this. I hope you'll hear my call and open your heart again. Because no one in this world deserves to be rejected.

Going too fast

WHEN I SAW YOU, YOU DIDN'T HAVE THE TIME,
YOU WERE IN A HURRY, YOU HAD SO MANY IMPORTANT
THINGS TO DO

THIS IS WHAT I'D HAVE LIKED TO TELL YOU… IF WE'D HAD
MORE TIME, TO TALK DEEPLY AND SINCERELY…

…I WOULD PROBABLY HAVE STARTED BY TELLING YOU
THIS STORY.

Once upon a time there was a little boy whose father was a feared monarch. Terribly busy with his duties, the King had entrusted the education of his son to a tax collector. However, it turned out that he was very strict and often punished the young prince. At nightfall, classes ended and the child returned to his room, often looking sad and desperate. This was still the case on the day our story begins, when the child-prince collapsed on his bed, tears in his eyes and said to himself: "What a cruel life a child has. Not only do you have to learn all these boring things, but you are also mistreated by teachers. But why on earth does time go by so slowly? How happy I'd be if I could grow up in one go with a magic wand".

When he woke up, he was surprised to discover a shiny reel of silk by his side. He started at it for long minutes, not knowing what to think, and when he decided to pick it up, a cavernous voice emanated from the reel and spoke these words to him:

"Take care my boy and listen carefully to what I say. I may look like a bobbin, but in fact I am much more than that. My silk thread represents every day of your life, minute by minute, my thread unwinds and unwinds. So the bobbin has an end, like your life, which will also come to an end. Last night you wished you could hasten the course of your life: I give you the power to do so. Unwind my silk thread, and time will speed up, your days will run out. But remember, my prince, that my thread is in perpetual motion, so you won't be able to stop time, let alone go backwards."

Transfixed by what he had just heard, the prince contemplated the reel, fascinated and pensive. He was greatly tempted to touch it to verify its omen. Somewhat anxious and as if to attenuate the effect of his impulse, he declared solemnly: "I'm going to pull a few centimetres of thread so that a day can pass."

And the thread was pulled... and as the reel had announced, his day passed before him in a flash and he found himself on his bed the next evening at the same time.

But the boy was still not satisfied with his fate; in his heart of hearts he was thinking:

"I'm well on my way; I don't mind losing a day. I'm still a child after all, forced to obey my master". And taking the reel in his hands he decreed:

"I want to be a grown-up, a grown-up man who is no longer accountable to anyone!".

No sooner had he started to unwind the thread than he metamorphosed and became a man, almost instantly. A beard framed his face and he was comfortably seated on a throne: he was now the monarch. Ministers and courtiers were busy around him and kept him busy with affairs of state. At first the prince, now a king, was delighted, but when he asked for news of his parents, he was told that they had died.

The king then began to cry his eyes out because he realised that he would never see them again. To console him, the courtiers encouraged him to marry, which he agreed to. An ambassador was sent to ask the monarch of the neighbouring kingdom for the hand of his daughter, who was reputed to be very beautiful.

But the ambassador was slow to return and the king began to lose patience. He ran to fetch the magic reel and ordered it to "unwind the thread of my days, the thread of my life". And immediately the long-awaited queen appeared at his side. Yet that was not enough; the king wanted children and once again he resorted to the reel, which granted his wish.

This time the infant's crying exasperated him, and with an angry face, the monarch cried out: "What good is a child who cries and eats all day like a small animal! I want to be able to talk to my son and teach him the art of war!".

He swiftly unwound the precious reel a little more and in this way continued to follow the rhythm of his unsatisfied desires, abusing his power by unwinding the thread... until he was an old man. Infirm and bedridden, the king tried to slow down time by summoning his memories, recalling the successive stages of his existence. He had to face the fact that time was continuing to eat away at his life, with no truce or respite.

Then, in desperation, he grabs the reel and, as one whispers a secret to someone, whispers to it: "Now that my life is coming to an end, I bow down before you, O reel, and beg you to grant me a reprieve and suspend time".

The reel had swapped its cavernous voice for a warm and melodious timbre, and it replied: "Your plea cannot move me, wretched prince, it is inadmissible. You have burnt your life; your laziness and impatience have got the better of you. Have you ever made the slightest effort to obtain anything? Have you ever cared about doing good deeds? It is your punishment to see yourself as you are in this mirror I hold before you".

The prince who had become king perished the next morning. As for his son, he abdicated his throne and devoted his life to philosophy, which he taught throughout his life at the university.

• • •

Jeff is married with three children and works in a bank near Paris. One weekday evening, as Jeff was coming home late, as usual, he was stopped at his door by Leo, his youngest son, aged six:

"Say daddy"
"Yes," Jeff replied.
"Where have you been?" continued the toddler.
"What do you think?" replied Jeff tersely. He was tired and still stressed from his day at the office.
"You were at the office," said the child with a broad smile, "how much money did you earn?"
Surprised by this question, Jeff froze and replied: "What bloody kind of question is that? Why are you asking me this?".

The child, in a natural tone of voice, said, "I want you to tell me. Please, Daddy".
Jeff paused, looked up to the sky and taking Leo in his arms answered: "I didn't know you were so materialistic but since you insist, I earn 25.35 euros gross per hour, and since I suppose my son, the tax inspector, wants to know everything, that's 20 euros net per hour plus dust! Are you happy now, can I go inside and relax?". Jeff was smiling now, in the end amused by this exchange. As soon as his back was turned, Léo cried out "Daddy, daddy, can you give me ten euros?".

Jeff suddenly lost his calm, and racked with tiredness he replied loudly: "No, my little man, I don't know what kind of game you're playing, but I'm starting to get really angry! What are all these questions anyway? That's not like you, Leo! Go to your room, I'm not happy". Looking sheepish, Leo obeyed.

An hour later, Jeff was overcome with remorse; he hardly ever raised his voice to his children, especially Leo, his youngest. "After all, what's the harm in asking his father for ten euros? Poor baby, I'm going to end up traumatising him with my mood swings!". Taking the ten euros out of his pocket, Jeff rushed to Leo's room and approached the toddler, "Here, Leo, here are the ten euros you asked me for". Leo, without even taking the money Jeff was handing him, rushed between his legs as was his habit when he was happy.

Curious, Jeff asked: "But tell me, what are you going to do with that money Leo?"
Suddenly looking more serious, Leo said: "Daddy, I had ten euros in my piggy bank, now it's 20 euros, that's an hour of your work, you told me. Can I give it to you so that you can have breakfast with me tomorrow morning?"

Jeff held Leo tight, hiding the tears that had come to his eyes.

• • •

Near the coast of Santo Domingo, a small fishing boat was returning to the port with several tuna that had just been caught by Rodrigue, a young fisherman. A rich European investor who was walking around the port saw the beautiful cargo and approached the boat and its young fisherman.
"How big are your tuna, how long did it take you to catch them?".
"Two hours of my time" replied Rodrigue who was proud at his catch that day, meaning he could sell his fish at auction and bring

back a few morsels for dinner that evening with his friends and family.

"But why did you return to the port then? You could have caught double or triple the amount of tuna if you'd had worked all day?" wondered the rich investor.

"This catch is more than enough for my needs and those of my family", replied the young fisherman as he unloaded his cargo.

The European then asked:

"But how do you spend the rest of the day?"

"I take a nap, I play with my children, I go to see friends. In the evening I play cards and sing. We drink beer and play music."

The European interrupted the fisherman and said to him:

"Listen to me: I studied at Cambridge University, I'm a wealthy investor and I can help you. The next thing you should do is to fish for longer, maybe two or three more hours. With the profits from this, you could buy a bigger fishing boat, buy nets and recruit a small crew. With the money earned, you could quickly buy a second boat and so on, until you have your own fleet. You could become quite the entrepreneur if you wanted to. By being smart, you could even cut out the middlemen and negotiate directly with the factory that buys your fish, and even one day open your own factory, or even buy something I've heard of – factory boats. You could then leave your small village and move to a big city and even move abroad, perhaps to London or Paris, where you would run your whole business."

The fisherman thought and asked:

"How long would it take?"

"About 20 years," replied the wealthy investor.

"And what would I do next?" asked the young fisherman.

"Well that's when things get interesting – when the time is right, you'll float your company on the stock exchange. You'll then earn millions by selling your shares. Of course, you won't sell them all. You'll keep some of them for an annuity."

"Millions, an income? But what would I do with all that money?"

"Well then you can retire, enjoy life, live in a small coastal village of Santo Domingo, take a nap, play with your children, go see your friends and in the evening you can drink beer and play music!!".

• • •

What if you took the time to breathe, to see, to hear, to touch? What if you took the time to stop and let the sun caress your face and warm your body? I know you love the fast life: money, power, fame, competition, projects, passions, girls, boys, etc. I know you love to move fast. There are so many reasons to run, to want to go fast. But when you do so, sometimes you forget to enjoy the moment. You want to have accomplished things, but without taking the time and taking pleasure in doing them.

• • •

The trees have kept some lingering sun in their branches,
Veiled like a woman, evoking another time,
The twilight passes, weeping. My fingers climb,
Trembling, provocative, the line of your haunches.
My ingenious fingers wait when they have found
The petal flesh beneath the robe they part.
How curious, complex, the touch, this subtle art–
As the dream of fragrance, the miracle of sound.
I follow slowly the graceful contours of your hips,
The curves of your shoulders, your neck, your unappeased
breasts.
In your white voluptuousness my desire rests,
Swooning, refusing itself the kisses of your lips.

RENÉ VIVIEN, THE TOUCH, 1903

• • •

Are you familiar with Epicure and his philosophy? Don't you sometimes feel like becoming a leaf that blows in the wind? That present moment, fleeting but so full of sensations. If you take the time to listen to your senses, you'll see that a second can be as long as an hour, so full it is of sensations. Pay attention, concentrate, think about what is happening in the here and now. It's a sensual discovery of the beauty of things, people and the world. It's like a prayer.

• • •

Don't ask (we're not to know) what end, Miranda,
the gods intend for you, for me; nor squander your mind
with horoscopes. Do better: let what will be, be.
Jove may grant winters yet or deem this year's your last
that wears the wide Tyrrhenian sea out on the brawny side
of cliffs. Be wise: have wine and prune the bough
of long hopes to short minutes. Even now as we speak here,
devouring time speeds on. Harvest this day*
and take no stock in dawn.

HORACE, TRANSLATION LECONTE DE LISLE, 1873

• • •

Are you mindful? If you want, I can help you find out. Mindfulness is the art of being present in the world. If you want to try it, start with a meal. Pay attention to the smell of each food, its shape and colour. Then when you put it in your mouth, pay attention to its taste and texture. Pay attention to the sensations that come from your palate, your cheeks, your tongue. Did you know that each part of your tongue is made to detect certain flavours? Take the time to really feel everything.

_____

* Carpe Diem

If you are in love, take the time to look at the one you love. Stop talking and just look at them. Observe their figure, observe their face. Listen to the sound of their voice. Feel the vibration of their whole body as they speak. Take the time to smell the different parts of their body. Take the time, when you caress their skin, to feel its texture, its warmth, its moisture. Mindfulness is a particularly sensual moment because all the senses are awakened.

When in this state, you'll discover some extraordinary sensations. You'll even be able to create silence within yourself. I'm sure you sometimes get tired of hearing that little inner voice reminding you of your obligations and problems. Mindfulness allows you to detach from consciousness, to return to a simpler and more primitive relationship with the world. Imagine an animal in the forest, on the lookout for what is happening. This is the state you are in when you achieve mindfulness.

If you are lucky, you'll be able to experience a connection with the world. Instead of feeling like a separate entity, you'll then feel connected to everything, as if part of the same whole, as if you somehow belong to the same family. Freud calls this feeling, the oceanic feeling. You feel it when you are swimming naked in the ocean or when you've just made love. Then you are fully connected to your senses.

• • •

"Did I use my time well?"

TITUS

• • •

As we grow older, we become aware of the importance of time. At twenty, you can spend your time doing anything and everything. We are under the illusion that time is an infinite resource, as the final deadline seems so far away, and we let ourselves believe that we will live forever. But then... then we realise that an hour, a day, a week is an eternity. We no longer want to waste these precious seconds on trivialities that don't contribute to our happiness or to the happiness of the people we love.

Old age teaches us to choose the books we read, the people we meet, the places we visit etc. If you are aware that your life is limited and that time passes quickly, then you'll only do the things that are really important to you and you won't waste time on suffering or giving yourself grief.

• • •

- To find out the value of a year, ask the student who has failed an important exam.
- To find out the value of a month, ask the mother who brought a child into the world too early.
- To find out the value of a week, ask the publisher of a weekly magazine.
- To find out the value of an hour, ask the lovers who are waiting to see each other again.
- To find out the value of one minute, ask the person who missed his train.
- To find out the value of a second, ask someone who has lost a loved one in an accident.
- To find out the value of a millisecond, ask the person who won a silver medal at the Olympic Games.

Time waits for no one. Gather every moment you have left and it will be of great value. Share them with the right people and these moments will be even more precious.

Being critical of our loved ones

WHEN I SAW YOU, WE SPENT A LOT OF TIME CRITICISING
SOME OF THE PEOPLE WE KNOW

I'VE BEEN THINKING ABOUT THAT, AND HERE'S WHAT
I'D LIKE TO TELL YOU... NOW I'VE REALISED THAT
WE WERE WRONG...

...I WOULD PROBABLY HAVE STARTED BY TELLING YOU
THIS STORY ABOUT OUR NEIGHBOURS.

Once there was a woman who had just retired. As she now had time to herself during the day, the next day she took the time to look out the window, something she hadn't done for a long time, since she used to get up very early. She then saw her neighbour in the building across the street, a young student, hanging out her clothes on the balcony. "Look," she said to her husband, "how dirty her laundry is". "She must not know how to do her laundry... maybe she needs me to show her".

In the days that followed, whenever the neighbour was hanging out her washing, the woman would make the same remark. Her husband, who was naturally silent, listened to her without saying a word... A fortnight later, the woman was surprised to suddenly see her neighbour's laundry sparkling white. "Look," she told her husband, "our neighbour's finally learned how to do her laundry. I wonder who taught her. I ran into her in the street the other morning, but I didn't dare tell her. It's none of our business after all".

Her husband raised his head and said, "No one! I just took the time to wash our dirty windows".

. . .

In ancient Greece, Socrates taught and received disciples and fellow philosophers every day. One day one of them came to him and said:

"Do you want to know what I've just learned about one of your disciples?"

"No, I don't", replied Socrates. At least before you reveal this secret, I'd like you to give a test about what you are about to tell me.

"A test?" asked his fellow philosopher.

"Yes, a test. This test is called the test of the three sieves."

"Okay", said his fellow philosopher, who was eager to reveal his secret.

"The first sieve is that of Truth.

Are you sure what you want to tell me is true? Have you taken the time to check it?"

"No, I must confess that I only heard about it... from one of my friends."

"All right," added Socrates. "So you're not sure this information is true.

Now you'll use a second sieve, the sieve of Kindness.

Is what you want to tell me about my disciple something good about him?"

"No; quite the contrary, it's something that does him no credit!"

"So you're about to tell me a story about one of my disciples which will cause him harm without being certain that it is true.

Now you'll use the third sieve, the sieve of Usefulness.

Is what you want to tell me going to be useful?"

"I couldn't say that either," added the fellow philosopher.

"If this information is not true, useful or good for this man, why do you want to tell me?"

• • •

Gossip is as crispy as crisps, as delicious to hear as it is to tell. But in the same way as crisps that are fatty and salty foods that do our health no good at all, gossip and rumours often do a lot of harm to people, and this harm is unnecessary. If you have compassion for others and sincerely wish them well, you should not gossip or rumour about them. The next time a friend tells you a story, do the three sieves test.

• • •

Sometimes I've noticed that it is difficult to refrain from criticising, judging or spreading rumours. I've noticed that this happens when we have nothing more to say, so we talk about others. I believe that in a way these words are meant to bring us closer together. By criticising others, we strengthen our bonds. In this way, we feel that we are the same, that we are on the right side, on the side of those who share the same values and the same ways of looking at things... But this is to the detriment of others.

• • •

"Criticism is a tax that envy levies on merit."

DUKE OF LÉVIS

• • •

I must admit, if I criticise others, it is because I'm jealous. I find out that one of my friends has been successful in this or that field, that he went on a trip that I couldn't make, that he won a lot of money... I'd like to be happy for him, but strangely enough, instead of being happy, I'm jealous. I feel I've got nothing interesting going on in my life, that I don't have as many opportunities or possibilities. So I have negative feelings towards them.

• • •

"The pleasure of criticism takes away from us the pleasure of being touched by very fine things"

JEAN DE LA BRUYÈRE

• • •

I believe the greatest bulwark against criticism, judgement and envy is success in life. If you identify your goals, act and achieve what you want to achieve in your heart of hearts, then you will no longer feel jealousy or envy. The only way to be good to others is to succeed in life. I've now decided that I'll never judge others negatively again. It's hard, but I've made this decision and I hope with all my heart that you'll be able to make the same one.

• • •

"Criticism is the power of the powerless."

ALPHONSE DE LAMARTINE

• • •

When you criticise, you exercise your power. As spectators we observe something and we say: it is not beautiful, it is not good, it is bad, it is unprofessional... But in so doing, we forget to see that this judgement is only the result of our thoughts and not of a reality or a truth. It is a mere perception, something which is relative. We must never forget this, because otherwise we risk hurting those who act and are trying to offer us something by giving the best of themselves.

• • •

One day, a man began to criticise the wise man of the village. Whenever he spoke to someone, he would complain about his attitude.

A few months later, when he began to get to know the wise man better, he realised his mistake and went to ask his forgiveness. He said, "Ask me anything you want, and I will do it to make it up to you."

The wise man was full of compassion. He simply said to him: "Fetch your pillow, go into your garden, tear it up and let the feathers scatter on the wind." The man did not even try to understand, but did what he was told. Then he returned to the wise man.

"Have you forgiven me now?" he asked.
"Not quite. Now I'd like you to go and pick up all the feathers from your pillow," replied the wise man.
"But that's impossible!" exclaimed the man, "the wind has scattered them all!"
"Well, it is as difficult to right the wrongs you have caused by your words as it is to retrieve the feathers scattered by the wind. Your words have also taken their path..."

• • •

For a long time, I failed to measure the impact of our words. Whenever we say something negative about something or someone, we help make the world a little darker. We think it's not serious or important but in fact our words have consequences. And afterwards, it's not always easy to right the wrong that has been done. That's why I suggest that the next time we speak, we try to always be positive about the world around us.

．．．

We must realise that our criticisms are also the fruit of our unfulfilled desires. Wouldn't the worker who criticises the lazy like to permit himself a few hours of idleness from time to time? Is not the brave man who mocks the coward also tempted to flee from time to time? And wouldn't the righteous man who criticises adultery like to fool about from time to time? All criticism is violence against others. But all criticism is also violence against oneself.

Our virtues can become prisons. And because we cannot escape them, being too eager to respect certain principles, we denounce those who are free. And criticism serves to maintain difference, so be free from time to time. If you are strong, become weak. If you are serious, fill yourself with wonder. If you are hard-working, be lazy. These experiences will make you grow. You'll understand your loved ones better and you'll be more forgiving to them and therefore to yourself.

．．．

Once two nomadic friends were crossing one of the hottest deserts on earth.
At one point during their trip, they had an argument. The first one slapped the second one. The latter, in pain, did not answer. He knelt on the ground and wrote in the sand:

"Today my best friend slapped me".

They continued on their way until they reached an oasis. There they were able to water their camels and wash themselves. The water was deeper than expected and the man who had been slapped could not swim. He almost drowned, but his friend pulled him out.

After taking a breath, he looked for a stone. Then he took a nail and a small hammer and carved on the stone:

"Today my best friend saved my life".

The one who had slapped him and saved him from drowning then asked him: "When I slapped you, you wrote on the sand, and now you have carved a stone. Why did you decide to do this?"

His best friend replied: "When someone hurts us, we must write it in the sand, where the winds of forgiveness will blow it away. But when someone does good for us, we must carve it in stone, so that nothing can erase it".

• • •

I'd like to ask your forgiveness. Because to be honest, I've sometimes spoken ill of you. I didn't mean any harm, but I did. I was wrong and I ask you to please let the wind blow my words away. If you have done the same, it's not a big deal – I forgive you. Now I know that we'll think twice before we say anything about someone. We'll be more careful because we know the impact our behaviour has on the world and on people.

Being angry

IN OUR LAST INTERVIEW YOU TOLD ME ABOUT
SOMEONE WHO HAD MADE YOU REALLY ANGRY ...
YOU WERE BESIDE YOURSELF, YOU WERE LIVID...

HERE'S WHAT I'D HAVE LIKED TO TELL YOU...
TO SOOTHE THE FIRE THAT BURNS IN YOU...
AND TRANSFORM THIS ENERGY INTO STRENGTH...

...I WOULD PROBABLY HAVE STARTED BY TELLING YOU
THIS STORY.

One day, in an Indian tribe, two brothers fought so hard their father had to separate them. They were fighting because one had accused the other of stealing one of his toys. The father sat them down and offered them a piece of dried meat. Then he said to them: "My sons, let me tell you this story. I too sometimes feel anger towards other people. But anger always wears out the person who feels it. Anger does not hurt the enemy. Anger is like a poison that you swallow hoping that the other person will repent."

He continued: "Inside every man and woman live two wolves. The first one is good to them and never does them any harm. On the contrary, it gives them strength. Most of the time it is as gentle as a lamb. It only fights when necessary, when it is useful, and he does it fairly. And when he fights, he does so with determination, but never with brutality or violence.

The wolf has a fine and subtle intelligence. It is a wise and courageous wolf.

The other wolf is full of anger and aggression. The slightest thing that goes wrong, the smallest obstacle, the smallest frustration throws him into fits of rage. He can fight anyone, all the time, for no reason, and without it adding anything to his life. He cannot think properly and use his intelligence, because he is blinded by his anger. He does not seek to enrich his life bur rather seeks to destroy those who have hurt or offended him.

Sometimes it's difficult to live with these two wolves inside you, because both of them want to dominate your mind." The two young brothers looked their father in the eye. "Which one of them wins, father?".

The father smiled and replied softly: "The one I feed."

• • •

Once upon a time there was a captain who had a large black moustache, which he maintained with great care, and of which he was very proud. The captain liked to make jokes to his nieces, who were mischievous little girls, and loved him dearly. One day, his nieces found an old French cheese, which was quite runny and smelly, in the captain's cellar. During the night, they entered the captain's room and brushed the cheese on his moustache, so that a disgusting smell immediately spread throughout the room.

When the captain got up at dawn, he couldn't help but wince. "But what a stink there is in this room!" he shouted, blocking his nostrils. Then he set off in search of the cause of the stench. He started sniffing his pillow. "Ugh... this pillow stinks!" And he threw it in the garbage. He did the same with his bedsheets, with a small rug and even with his own bed, which also stank terribly.

Even the furniture smelled bad and he felt like throwing it out the window.

He opened the window to try to ventilate the room but when he breathed in the fresh air from the garden, he could still smell the same disgusting smell. The garden with its pretty flowers, the surrounding meadows, even the distant sea, all stank horribly. "This world disgusts me!" he shouted. And all his day went on like that until he finally realised the trick his nieces had played on him and that the bad smell was not from the world but simply from his moustache[*]!

• • •

One day, there was a great war between two great kingdoms of Japan. Thousands of men and women clashed In each of these great kingdoms, among them great warriors who were champions of war and were called Samurai.

And then, just as the spring sun melts the snow and makes the cherry trees blossom, peace returned between the two kingdoms. A new era began. Those who had been great warriors had to surrender their weapons. One of them was called Ishiro.

Once the war was over, Ishiro didn't know what to do with himself. In the morning when he got up, he felt the urge to go to war. In the afternoon, he felt the desire to go to war. And at night, he felt like going to fight. But there was no more war.

Ishiro fell into a terrible depression. He started drinking and became angry. All day long he argued with his wife, children and neighbours. In the evening he hung out in the taverns, drinking and arguing with the other customers.

---

* We owe this story to Robert Mac Donald.

He often got into fights. He didn't come home until dawn, when he would start arguing again with his wife, children and neighbours. Ishiro never learned to live in peace and this eternal fight only ended when he died.

• • •

"When someone makes you angry, know that it is your own thought that makes you angry."

EPICTETUS

• • •

"Fear leads to anger, anger leads to hatred, hatred leads to suffering."

MASTER YODA

• • •

Anger arises in three types of situations. When the situation is unfair, when another person allows themselves to do things they're not allowed to do, and when one of your desires is frustrated. Anger is meant to make you act to change the situation. You need to make the situation fairer, stop the person who acted against you from doing the same thing again and satisfy your desire. So anger is an energy that invites you to change the world to restore balance.

Some people are still angry. They don't have the life they would like to have but they don't make the effort to change the world around them. They prefer to be angry because anger is like a drug. Other people are always angry because they don't know how to experience other emotions. These people are warriors who have only known war and do not know how to live in times of peace, like Ishiro. There are times when fighting others and the world is useless.

Anger is a sign that you need to change something in your life or in your relationships with others. If you change nothing, then the anger will grow until it consumes you, but while anger is a sign, it should never be a means or an end. You can only change the world through work and dialogue. And if the world or the people you surround yourself wife don't change and your anger remains, then you have to leave and escape the source of your anger. You'll find peace away from them.

• • •

"Anger means three things:
1. We are upset because we are not getting our needs met,
2. We are blaming someone or something else for
not getting what we want,
3. We are about to speak or act in such a way that
will almost guarantee we will not get what we need,
or that we will later regret."

MARSHALL B. ROSENBERG

• • •

Anger has three levels of power:

- The first level of power of anger is annoyance. You feel irritated by a person or situation. Your heart speeds up slightly. You feel a bit of aggression building up in you.
- The second level of power is called anger. Your heart is accelerating noticeably. You feel tension in your muscles. Your face begins to turn red. You feel something in her belly, like a ball. You are aggressive. You feel like arguing. You say unpleasant and harsh words to hurt and upset someone.

- The third level of power of anger is rage, when you lose control of yourself. You speak words without thinking about the consequences. You feel the desire to destroy. Your mind becomes veiled, your behaviour and reactions become irrational. You may commit acts of violence against others. Your muscles are stretched to the limit. Your face is red. Your jaw is tight. This is the reaction of a wounded animal. Rage can lead you to commit irreparable acts of extreme violence.

. . .

Once upon a time there was a little girl who was never happy and was always complaining. One day her mother gave her a bag of tacks. She said: "Take these tacks and whenever you get angry, stick one in this wooden plank.

By evening, the little girl had stuck forty-two tacks in the board. The days passed and the little girl stuck fewer tacks in each day. She had understood that sticking a tack in a hardwood was harder than getting angry.

One day, the little girl managed to stay calm for an entire to. She had no more reason to stick tacks wooden plank, so her mother asked her to remove every single tack she had stuck in the plank of wood.

The girl obeyed and removed all the tacks. She then called her mother who said: "That's fine my child, come closer now and look at all these holes, the tacks have left traces that can never disappear."

The same thing happens in life. When you say things in anger, think of it as a tack that you stick into a person's heart. You can always take it out, but there will always be a hole.

You may regret what you said and apologise, but the wound will remain forever. Next time, before you let your anger get the better of you, think back to those tacks, their points and the wounds they will leave in the hearts of the people you love.

• • •

The problem with anger is that it leads us to react inappropriately or disproportionately to a situation. It helps to block communication with those involved. If there is a conflict, anger will cause you to hurt the person you are talking to by using hurtful words against them. If the person is hurt, then they will have no desire to resolve the conflict, which is why you should never speak or react in anger. Wait until the anger dissipates.

• • •

"You vanquish anger when you keep quiet."

EGYPTIAN PROVERB

• • •

When anger approaches, don't try to control it. Watch it flow into your body. You'll see, it starts in your belly and spreads everywhere. Let it fill you up completely by observing it like a spectator contemplating the beauty of a storm or a devastating torrent. Watch how it changes your perceptions, your feelings, your attitude, your posture, your gaze, your physiology. Observe in silence without moving and learn from yourself because at that moment, anger is giving you a lesson in wisdom.

Now try to understand why you felt this anger. Did you feel betrayed? Did you encounter a situation that you felt was unfair? Did someone deprive you of the satisfaction of one of your most cherished desires? Did someone repeat something that usually makes you angry? Try to understand and verbalise why you felt this anger in one sentence. Say: "I felt angry because…". And then you'll have understood the origin of this storm.

Then find a situation which is the opposite to the one you encountered at that time. For example, if someone lied to you, think of a time when someone told you the truth. If someone did an injustice to you, think of someone who was fair to you. If someone has prevented you from satisfying your desires, think of someone who has fully satisfied them. When you find yourself in this situation, really think about it. You should then feel a deep sense of peace of mind and well-being.

Control your mind and direct your attention to that memory that brought you such peace of mind yesterday. You'll then discover that you are the master of your emotions. Through the power of memory, you can change the emotions you are experiencing and provoke anger or peace of mind in yourself depending on what you want to achieve. In the days that follow, have fun making anger come and go. Have fun bringing joy and peace of mind into you and making it go away. This way you'll learn to control your emotions.

• • •

Anger is like a burning fire which can be destructive or, on the contrary, become an extraordinary source of energy. Think of the fire that drives your car, runs trains and flies planes. Without fire nothing would be possible in the same way that without anger some changes would be impossible. Take the fire of anger, channel it within you and direct it towards a positive transformation of your life. You'll see that anger, instead of being the driver of destruction will become the driver of transformation.

• • •

Maybe sometimes you make other people angry. If you make other people angry, then question your own behaviour. Men and women react differently to situations, so it's unfair to repeat an act that makes someone angry. Maybe you think the person is wrong to get angry. Maybe you think there's no reason to get angry. Don't judge, just change your behaviour.

• • •

"He that quenches anger quenches a fire;
he that stirs up anger shall be the first to perish
in the flames."

HAZRAT ALI

• • •

A lecturer in psychology is giving a course on emotions during a seminar:
"Today, I'm going to introduce you to the different stages of anger" he says. Then he takes his mobile phone, dials a random number and says:
"Hello sir, I'd like to speak to George, please?"
"You must have got the wrong number; my name is not George."
He looks at the conference participants and adds:
"This is the phase of annoyance."
He picks up his phone and dials the number again. The gentleman, indeed a little upset, answers:
"You just called me; I told you my name wasn't George. I don't know anyone named George!"
The speaker then dials a third time, then a fourth, then a fifth... until the angry gentleman ends up calling him names. He turns to the audience and says:

"This is now the stage of anger. But there is yet a further stage."
He picks up his mobile phone and dials the number again.
"Hello Sir, I'm George. Has anyone called to leave a message?"

• • •

If one day I make you angry, come and tell me right away. I'll apologise immediately and stop behaving as I did. No doubt, I had failed to pay attention or that I didn't think I was doing anything wrong. You know, we don't always know how to behave. We can make mistakes or errors. I wish you well above all. Also, I don't want you to be angry because I know that anger is bad for your health. I want to see you serene, well and at peace.

Refusing help

I HAVE A LOT OF RESPECT FOR YOU BECAUSE I KNOW
YOU'RE CURRENTLY GOING THROUGH A DIFFICULT
PERIOD IN YOUR LIFE.

I KNOW YOU WANT TO GET THROUGH THIS ON YOUR
OWN, WITHOUT THE HELP OF YOUR LOVED ONES...

BUT THIS IS WHAT I'D LIKE TO SAY TO YOU...
SO THAT YOU OPEN YOUR HEART AND ACCEPT
THE PRECIOUS HELP THAT IS OFFERED TO YOU.

...BUT FIRST I'D LIKE TO TELL YOU THIS STORY.

On the borders of India, in the kingdom of Agra, young Aladdin
leads the carefree life of a street kid. Rather than receiving
alms, he prefers to steal what he needs to eat from the market
stalls. The city is ruled by a Sultan whose daughter, a princess, is
waiting to find Love to get married. Every day she dismisses the
rich princes who come to ask her to marry them so that they can
inherit her father's rich kingdom in return. One day, to explore
the world outside the palace where she has lived in seclusion
since she was a child, the princess decides to escape and venture
into the city but has a run-in with some soldiers. She is saved in
extremis by the young Aladdin. While Aladdin shows the Princess
his life, the Grand Vizier recognises Aladdin as the "diamond of
innocence" that will enable him to get hold of the magical lamp
hidden in a secret cave.

The grand vizier disguised as a beggar convinces Aladdin to come with him to the cave. He sends Aladdin to fetch an oil lamp, but his tame monkey cannot resist the urge to steal a gem, causing the cave to collapse. Aladdin then finds himself locked in the dark in the depths of a cave lost in the desert. Being in the dark, he tries to light the oil lamp and rubs it with a cloth, which is when a flamboyant genie appears, both funny and powerful, who offers to grant him three wishes. The genie will save Aladdin, make him rich, help him triumph over the Grand Vizier and finally win over the princess seduced by his sincere love. The last of his wishes will free the Genie who served him so well.

• • •

Among the people around you, as in the story of Aladdin, are genies who have the power to make your life easier. All you need to do is dare to ask them for help. Learn how to ask for help and you'll be surprised by the time and energy that others are able to devote to you. Nature is such that human beings prefer to help rather than be helped. So it's very easy to get help when you are in difficulty or when you want to achieve a difficult goal.

• • •

"Helping the wounded and the weak is what differentiates man from the animal. "

HUGO PRATT

• • •

The enemy of happiness and success is always the ego. But what exactly is the ego? The ego is that part of oneself that absolutely wants to exist and to master. When you have a problem, your ego rebels; at first, it tries to overcome the obstacle on its own because it wants to prove its power. But if it fails, then it can stubbornly try to solve a problem alone when it is impossible to do so. Asking for help means accepting its weakness and fragility. It means accepting its human condition.

• • •

"A man is never as big as when he is on his knees to help a child."

PYTHAGORAS

• • •

Human beings are naturally good, but sometimes they fail to see that you're in trouble. They're afraid to bother you or offend you by offering to help you. They're afraid that you'll tell them: "Mind your own business, I'm doing fine on my own!" Don't be afraid to ask others for help. For there is no greater honour you can do to a friend, no greater proof of trust you can give them than to open your heart when you're in difficulty to ask for their support and advice.

Helping gives meaning to one's life. What could be more beautiful than seeing another human being escape from danger or solve a difficult problem with our help? When you see someone who's doing well or better because of you, don't you feel immense satisfaction? Don't deny this privilege, pleasure and honour to the people you love. Let them be someone who matters in your life. Let them be a positive influence in your life. Doing that will make them happy.

• • •

"To live is to help to live.
You have to create other happiness
to be happy! "

RAOUL FOLLEREAU

• • •

Some people refuse help because they don't want to feel indebted, because accepting someone's help is, in a way, accepting the idea that one day we'll have to return the favour. It's like a debt! Others refuse because they feel that whoever asks for help is weak, yet It's exactly the opposite. He who asks for help is strong; h's strong because he's smart. He's strong because he knows that man is a social animal, that he is a being of relationships and cooperation.

• • •

Once a woman was walking down the street. She was careless and fell into a manhole cover that someone had left open.

– A nun passing by cried: "Madam, you must have committed a sin. Do you want me to hear your confession?".
– A scientist calculated the width and depth of the manhole as well as the falling speed.
– A journalist interviewed her to find out where it hurt, what had caused her to fall and sought to identify those responsible.
– A lawyer suggested that taking the perpetrators to court to seek damages.
– An insurer tried to sell her legal protection insurance so she could sue those responsible for this situation.
– A follower of Buddhism and transcendental meditation said to her: "This manhole is only in your mind, like your pain".
– A doctor threw a packet of powerful painkillers at her.

– A psychoanalyst suggested that it was probably a missed act, an unconscious impulse that had caused her to fall into that manhole.

– A therapist offered to help her heal her compulsion to fall into manholes and the phobia that would result from the accident.

– An optimist added: "You're only in pain; you're lucky, you could have been seriously injured in the fall".

– A pessimist added: "This fall is only the beginning of a long series of problems...".

– Then a child passed by in the street, and offered her his hand...

• • •

If you ever need to ask for help, you shouldn't necessarily look for someone competent. Instead, look for a human being who is sensitive to your difficulties and will be willing to help you. A good carer is first and foremost a humble person whose primary motivation is to be of service to others. Receiving help means, first of all, receiving compassion and then taking action to find a concrete solution to one's problems. This is the way to solve life's difficulties.

• • •

Help, I need somebody.
Help, not just anybody.
Help, you know I need someone, Help!

When I was younger, so much younger than today.
I never needed anybody's help in any way.
But now these days are gone, I'm not so self-assured.
Now I find I've changed my mind and I opened up the doors.

THE BEATLES, HELP, 1965

• • •

"To set fire to a forest, you need the help of the wind. "

TIBETAN PROVERB

• • •

In the midst of winter, a schoolteacher is helping the children get dressed before going to the playground. One of the children needs help getting his boots on, and after pushing, pulling, struggling and pushing back in all directions, the boots are finally put on. The child then says:

"They're the wrong way round, teacher."

Noticing that she has indeed got them the wrong way round, the schoolteacher removes them, with some difficulty. They're as difficult to remove as they were to put on. Then, once she has removed them, she puts them back on again. This time the child tells her:

"Actually, teacher, these aren't my boots!"

The schoolteacher stifles the anger she can feel rising up and her and restores her calm, which has been sorely tested:

"Why didn't you tell me this before?"

The child who has noticed that his teacher is upset, does not respond. He lets her take the boots off again before adding:

"Actually, they're not my boots, they're my brother's, but my mum told me I had to put them on."

Tears come to the schoolteacher's eyes. She takes a deep breath and struggles to put the boots back on the child, still with difficulty. Mission accomplished! Going that bit further, she helps the child put on his coat, wraps his scarf around his neck and asks him:

"Where did you put your gloves?"

"To avoid losing them," replies the child, "I put them in my boots."

• • •

I'm here, so if you need help just let me know. I won't judge you; I won't try to control your life; I won't try to do things you don't want to do. I'll accept this mission with humility. But I'll do everything I can to help you because you mean a lot to me and your happiness is one of the most important things for me. So if you're in trouble, you have my number, my email, my Skype, my Snap, my Facebook... Call and I'll answer you!

Facing a difficult problem

WHEN I SAW YOU, YOU WERE BEING FACED
WITH A VERY DIFFICULT PROBLEM TO SOLVE,
SO MUCH SO THAT YOU FELT POWERLESS

THAT'S WHAT I'D HAVE LIKED TO TELL YOU...
TO GET YOU TO COME UP WITH NEW SOLUTIONS
AND ESCAPE THIS IMPASSE...

...I WOULD PROBABLY HAVE STARTED BY TELLING YOU
THIS STORY.

A very long time ago, in a village in the land of the mountain people, there was a very poor farmer who had to repay a very large debt to an ugly old moneylender. The farmer was the father of a very pretty girl who the old moneylender found very attractive. So the old moneylender offered the farmer a deal. He would consider his debt paid off if he could marry his daughter. At first the farmer and his daughter refused this proposal. Then the old moneylender, who was also very clever, proposed that chance should decide their destiny.

He would place a white stone and a black stone in a bag. The girl would have to choose the stone, blindly.
1) If she chose the black stone then she would have to marry him, and her father's debt would be cancelled.
2) If she chose the white stone, she would not have to marry him, and her father's debt would be cancelled.

3) If she refused to choose a stone, her father would be arrested and thrown into prison.

In other words, the girl and her father had no choice but to participate in this perverse game.

Forced and coerced, the farmer and the old moneylender agreed so, muttering, the old moneylender picked up two stones on the path and threw them into a bag. The young girl noticed that he had picked up only two black stones. But she said nothing. The old moneylender handed the bag to the girl and asked her to choose one stone. What could she do to get out of this bind? If you'd been in her place, what would you have done?

1) The daughter should have refused to take a stone at the risk of seeing her father thrown in jail.

2) The daughter should have taken the two stones to reveal the deception of the old loan shark, but in this case, the old loan shark would have reported them to the police and her father would be thrown in jail.

3) The daughter should have taken the black stone without saying anything and agreed to marry the old loan shark and thus avoid her father's imprisonment.

What would you have done in the girl's place?

This is what she did:

She slipped her hand into the bag and took out a stone which she immediately let slip onto the path, left, without anyone being able to see it. The stone merged with the multitude of other stones on the ground.

"Ah, how stupid I am," exclaimed the girl. "But it doesn't matter; if I take the stone that is left out of the bag, we'll see which one I took first!"

As the remaining stone was black, the first stone had to be white. And as the old moneylender did not dare to reveal his ruse, the young girl finally turned this desperate situation to her advantage... Her father's debt was cancelled, and she didn't have to marry the old moneylender.

• • •

Even if you are faced with a problem that seems insoluble to you, remember that there is always a way to turn the situation to your advantage. Even the most desperate of situations, you can come out a winner. All it requires is imagination and creativity; it requires you to use all your intelligence (and sometimes the intelligence of those around you – many people are smarter than you), but always tell yourself it's possible. You just need enough time to find the right answer.

• • •

First riddle:

Every day of the week, a man crossed the border three times with his donkey, which was laden with two saddlebags full of worthless stones. The customs officer searched him and could not understand why the man was getting richer and richer.
He was sure he was mixed up in something...
What do you think the man was trafficking in?

Answer to this riddle:
The answer to this enigma is the name of the animal that perished after its masters a farmer and his son, were criticised. It was from this smuggler that they had bought the animal, for this smuggler was in fact a donkey trafficker...

• • •

If you agree, imagine that you're walking along a path which dins through a dark and black forest of fir trees, which are so close together that they don't let the light through. Something unhealthy is coming out of this forest, something that makes you feel uncomfortable. You're surrounded by thousands of dark and threatening fir trees which represent the problem you're facing. You can't see anything because of the trees. Your future seems as blocked as this black forest.

You walk on, and suddenly you come to a beautiful clearing. The ground is lined with green grass and colourful flowers, and purple butterflies are flying everywhere under a blue sky. In the centre of the clearing, a hot-air balloon is waiting for you; the red balloon, inflated with hot air, is ready to go. *Let's go!* You jump into the basket and drop anchor. Let's go! What a feeling of lightness as the balloon takes off among the trees. You shout with joy, waking up all the birds that start to sing.

The balloon rises, past the black trunks bristling with thorny branches. The higher you go, the more light there is, and the sun fills the sky with its warm light. In your head, you feel that everything is full of light, and now you're in the treetops from where you can see the whole forest which is both huge and tiny from above. You unhook the ballast that is slowing the balloon down and it starts to rise quickly. It's not a balloon, it's a spaceship, heading for the galaxy of solutions.

The balloon driven by the winds carries you towards your destiny over forests, lakes and meadows, over mountains and abysses. Now you are far away from the original forest, surrounded by a beautiful landscape. Your eyes look towards the horizon as the wind carries you close to the sea and gently gusts and caresses your shoulders. You observe the beauty of the world under your feet. Strangely enough, in the distance, a rainbow bridges the gap between heaven and earth.

The problem you were facing, which seemed like the end of the world, was in fact just a tiny obstacle on the long road of your life, which will be long and beautiful. And you'll be happy and successful because you are full of resources, talents and intelligence. If you find yourself facing an impassable wall, dig a hole to go under it; if you're lost, find a compass; if you have fallen into a hole, then climb out of it or build yourself a ladder. In your hands is the power to create your solution.[*]

• • •

"There are no problems; there are only solutions.
The mind or the man then invents the problem.
He sees problems everywhere."

ANDRÉ GIDE

• • •

"A problem without a solution is a problem badly posed."

ALBERT EINSTEIN

• • •

One day, three young girls came to a wise woman.
"We have a problem with one of our friends," they said. She is authoritarian, aggressive and won't be contradicted. We're fed up with her."
"She needs to be told, said the first girl. We're going to tell her nicely that the way she's behaving is bothering us; then we can convince her to change her character, and if that doesn't work, we'll be even harder on her. Nothing will go wrong, even if we have to be aggressive in turn."
"I'm afraid," said the second girl, "that it will create conflict. I must admit, I don't like conflict. It's better to avoid it because it's exhausting."

---

[*] This text is taken from the book: *Hypnosis: the key to happiness* (2017).

"And also she's our friend," said the third girl. "I don't think we should try to change her; we have to accept her as she is."

"All three of you are right," said the woman. "Confronting someone to try to change them is not a good thing. Because if it doesn't work, you risk turning into a bully. You must let go and choose another tactic: avoidance, distance or flight."

"I don't agree," said the first girl. "To run away is to be a coward. And it won't help her face up to her flaws."

"If it's fear of confrontation that causes you to flee," says the woman, "you're right to think that. But if you've done all you can to change things and it doesn't work, then continuing to confront each other makes no sense. Avoidance becomes a good choice."

"And there's a third option: acceptance. When an unpleasant reality cannot be changed or avoided, one must learn to accept it."

"That means giving up," said the second girl. "I don't agree with that. Because perseverance always pays off."

"Acceptance is not giving up," says the woman.

"What's the difference?" asked the third girl.

"If you can neither change things nor avoid them," said the woman, "you have to change yourself. Change what you expect from the situation, learn to accept and love things as they are. Doing this shows courage and intelligence."

"So whenever a reality does not correspond to our ideal, we have the choice between these three stances?" asked the second girl.

"Yes," said the woman. "You have the choice between confrontation, avoidance and acceptance. Or their dark side: violence, flight and resignation.

The choice is yours."

• • •

Second riddle:

All it takes is a yes or no for them to separate.

Answer:

The lips

I have little strength, but a lot of power,
I guard slums like palaces,
But if my master leaves,
You must make sure he takes me with him.

Answer:

The key

• • •

When faced with a difficult problem in your life, change your approach. Remember when you were a child you used to play puzzles. Remember how much fun you had playing these games. It was fun and exciting-sometimes unbearable when you couldn't figure them out. Life is a game; if you take it lightly, if you accept not to make every single event in your life into a drama, then you'll find pleasure in facing problems.

• • •

Third riddle:

A young married woman, abandoned by a husband who was always too busy with his job, is seduced and goes to spend the night at her lover's house across the river. To return home early the next day, before her husband returns from his trip, she has to cross the bridge again. But a dangerous madman blocks her way. She runs to find a boatman and asks him to take her across the river, but she has no money.

She explains and begs but he refuses to take her without being paid in advance. She then goes to find her lover and asks him for money, but he refuses in turn, without the slightest explanation. So she goes to find a single friend who lives on the same side of the street and who has always held an unrequited love for her. She tells him everything and asks him for money, but he refuses: she has disappointed him with her behaviour. After trying the ferryman again, she decides to cross the bridge. The madman kills her. Who is responsible?

Most people who answer this riddle say the lover or the madman or the boatman. If you agree, you're making the same mistake as these people. You're making what in psychology we call: the fundamental error of attribution. The fundamental error of attribution consists in attributing responsibility for an event or situation to people rather than to the context in which these people find themselves.

For example, a person suffers a road accident. It will be tempting to think: this person is responsible. They were probably driving carelessly or did not pay enough attention". Yet the problem may have been caused by the road, poorly maintained, a car of poor quality or with faulty brakes, or a wild animal that appeared out of nowhere. If the accident happened, it was not just because of the person, but because of a host of causes.

If you are faced with a difficult problem and you're looking for the cause of that problem, look for the cause in both people and circumstances, as circumstances often shape people's decisions. See the situation as a system, without judging people, and observe dispassionately what problems the system causes. By changing circumstances, you can influence people positively and solve their problem.

• • •

Oblique Strategies is a card game created by Brian Eno and Peter Schmidt in 1975. On each card is written a formula that can be open to different interpretations. The aim of the card game is to restart the creative process when blockages occur. I have drawn six cards from the deck* for you:

---

* Draw another card on: http://www.davidrolo.com/photo/strategies-obliques/

- Card 1: is it finished?
- Card 2: the band is the music.
- Card 3: infinitesimal gradations.
- Card 4: stupid enjoyment (?)
- Card 5: the most important thing is the most easily forgotten thing
- Card 6: short circuit (take the shortest route)

· · ·

If you are faced with a difficult problem, start by thinking about what the situation would be like if the problem got even worse. What would happen if the problem got worse? Behind the word "problem" is often "a change", and sometimes this change is impossible to prevent. If you first let the change happen in your mind, you'll let it happen all the easier in reality. Then your problem will disappear because you have let it become something else.

· · ·

If you want to solve a problem, start by identifying the causes of the problem. To do this, use the "five whys" technique. This technique involves asking the question "why" five times to identify the root cause of a problem. While writing this book, I had an accident. I was walking down the street and stumbled on a small step. I slid several metres and found myself lying on the ground in the middle of the street, which made a child laugh and scared an old lady.

1. Why did I fall?
Because I didn't pay attention.
2. Why didn't I pay attention?
Because I was preoccupied with my work?
3. Why was I preoccupied with my work?
Because I'm writing an exciting book on personal development...

4. Why am I writing this book?
Because I take a lot of pleasure in it.
5. Why do I enjoy it so much?
Because it makes me happy to help others and provide them with solutions.

In this case, the analysis of causes brought me back to my passion for writing, which is something I wouldn't want to change under any circumstances. So I just need to accept that I will fall down from time to time, making children laugh and scaring old ladies. If, however, the analysis of causes had pointed to something negative, like stress or fatigue, then I'd have had to change things in my life. I should have rested more to reduce my stress and fatigue. A problem can call for a change.

· · ·

"Adventure is just a romantic name for trouble."

LOUIS L'AMOUR

· · ·

1+1 = 3. So if you need help with a difficult problem, call me and we'll take the time to examine things calmly over a strong coffee. I'll give you my point of view, my opinion. Maybe I'll even have the audacity to give you some advice. But never forget: the solution always lies within you. Often you already know it, it's just that it's hard to accept! Trust your intuition. It's totally irrational, but that's often how you make the best decisions.

Losing self-confidence

NOW THAT I KNOW YOU WELL, I KNOW THAT YOU SOMETIMES LOSE CONFIDENCE IN YOURSELF.

...AND PRECISELY BECAUSE I KNOW WHO YOU REALLY ARE, I WANT TO TELL YOU HOW I FEEL, TO TELL YOU ALL THIS EXTRAORDINARY POTENTIAL THAT LIES WITHIN YOU AND WHICH MAKES YOU GREAT IN MY EYES.

NEXT TIME I'LL TELL YOU THESE THINGS AND I'LL PROBABLY START BY TELLING YOU THIS ANCIENT STORY.

In India, an ancient legend tells that there was a time when all men were gods and women were goddesses. But they abused their power so much that Brahma, the king of the gods, chose to remove them. To challenge them with patience and wisdom, he decided to hide this power in a place where it would be impossible to find. But the gods and goddesses could see all, so the problem he faced was finding a suitable hiding place. He therefore sought the advice of the wisest of his holy advisers.

The first holy advisor counsellor proposed: "You should hide the divine power of men and women deep in the earth."
But Brahma replied: "Men and women will dig, and they will find it".
The second holy advisor proposed: "we could throw their divine power into the deepest sea".

But Brahma replied: "No, for there will come a day when men and women will set out to explore the depths of the seas. And when that time comes, they will find it."

His holy advisors were at a loss – where could Brahma hide the divine power of men and women? Because men and women were very curious and determined: "We do not know where to hide this power", they told Brahma, "it seems that there is no place that men and women will not think of exploring."

Then Brahma said: "We're going to hide the divinity of men and women in a place they'll never think of looking; we'll hide it deep within themselves."

Legend has it that since that ancient time, men and women have travelled around the world in search of their divine power. They have explored the world and even the surface of the moon, climbed the highest mountains and plunged into the depths of the seas and oceans, in search of a treasure that actually lies deep within themselves*.

• • •

Sophie has just been promoted at work. She's happy and proud because it's thanks to all the work and energy she has given to her company over the last few years that she's being rewarded. Yet in her company, other employees do not see the situation in the same way. Rather than sharing her happiness and joy, eaten away by jealousy and envy, they start spreading awful rumours about Sophie.

"She got the job because she has pretty eyes. It wouldn't surprise me if she was... with the boss! She slept her way to the top!

---

* This story is based on the book: *Discover the Power Within You by Butterworth* (2000).

She's not qualified! She doesn't have enough experience! She's going to fail! Do you know how stupid she once was... and she hasn't even been punished". Around the coffee machine, each comment is more hurtful than the previous one.

That weekend, Sophie visits her antique dealer father and tells him that she has just been promoted. Her father immediately sees how happy she is, yet at the same time sees her sadness and bitterness. She should be happy and proud and feel strong, but the situation seems to have worn her down, so he questions her. She then reveals to him the attacks she has borne the brunt of since her promotion.

"I understand," said his father. "You're happy to be promoted, you think you deserve it, but you're hurt by the reactions of your colleagues... and if this continues you risk losing confidence in yourself... If you want, I suggest doing an experiment." Sophie accepts because she has great trust in her father who has always given her good advice. She knows he only wants the best for her. He loves her.

"Darling," her father asks her, "could you go to the antique market tomorrow morning and sell this vase? I've just restored it and I'd like to sell it. Please put it on sale for 70 euros."
"Seventy euros! That doesn't seem like much for this nice vase!" replied Sophie.
"Don't worry about it. I paid a certain price for it and that's the price I want. This will allow you to develop your selling skills."
The next day, Sophie goes to the antique market. All morning she tries to sell the vase. Unfortunately, no one shows up to buy it. Sophie, greatly disappointed, goes home and tells her father about her experience.
His father then added, without making any further comments: "Now, take this vase and visit the five antique dealers who work in this neighbourhood. But this time just ask them what they're willing to pay for the vase. Just ask the price. Don't sell the vase."

The first antique dealer offered her 400 euros, the second 500 euros... The fifth offered 1000 euros.

Sophie is greatly surprised. She doesn't understand what is going on, so she goes home and tells her father about her experience. He asks her: "Why do you think you couldn't sell this vase for 70 euros this morning?"

"Because I spoke to people who didn't know the origins of this vase and who didn't know its true value."

"And why did my colleagues in the antiques trade offer you so much money for it?"

"Because they're experts who know its exact value. They immediately saw how valuable it was."

"So now consider about your colleagues. Why do you give them the right to judge your worth? Are they experts in assessing your skills and what you can bring to your company?"

"No," replied Sophie, slightly nervous yet at the same time reassured.

"My darling, never let your heart be affected by the judgements of those who are not experts. Listen only to the judgements of professionals or experts in human nature. And you'll see that your value is far greater than you imagine."

• • •

A famous lecturer once began his seminar by showing a hundred-euro banknote. He asked the participants:

"Who'd like to own this note?". Many participants raised their hands. Then he said: "I'll give this 100 euro note to one of the participants, but first I'd like to do something with it." He took the banknote and crumpled it in his hand. And he asked again: "Do you still want this note?"

Just as many participants raised their hands.

"OK, but what happens if I do this?"

He threw the crumpled ball of the banknote on the floor and crushed it with the heel of his shoe. Then he jumped on it until it was so crumpled and dirty that it was unrecognisable.

And he asked again:

"Now who wants this note?"

Just as many participants raised their hands.

"Dear participants, you have just learned something very important... No matter what I do with this note, you still want it because its value has not changed. No matter what I do with it, it's still worth a hundred euros. So think of yourself, of your existence. There will be many times in your life when you'll be offended, rejected, soiled by people or events. You'll then feel that you're worthless, but in reality, as is the case with this banknote, your value will not have changed. A person's value does not depend on what they have done or not done. You'll always be able to start over and achieve your goals because your value will always remain intact no matter what happens."

• • •

"The value of a man is not measured by his money, status or possessions. The value of a man lies in his personality, wisdom, creativity, courage, independence and maturity. "

MARK W. B. BRINTON

• • •

You have a treasure within you. Perhaps you have not yet discovered it, but it is there. The first thing you need to do to find or regain your self-confidence is to go and find it. Get to know your values, your needs, your personality and your talents. Once you know them – and you will – you'll know who you are and what your destiny is. Then your self-confidence will be unshakeable. You'll be stronger than rock.

• • •

• • •

Self-confidence means accepting difficult or uncomfortable situations. It's all the easier to accept them when you know why. If you want self-confidence, remember the objective you have set yourself. You must never lose sight of this objective. It is the goal that keeps you going through life. It is the goal that catches you and prevents you from getting lost in the abyss if you fall. Keep your goal in sight. Become a seeker missile!

• • •

• • •

When you encounter a difficult situation, you are probably stressed, afraid, feeling bad... What makes the situation so uncomfortable is not the situation itself, it is your emotions, your thoughts, your feelings... It is never the situation you are running away from; it is how you feel about it. This means that if you train yourself to manage the situation, then the emotions, the thoughts, the sensations will calm down. It is through training that self-confidence is acquired.

• • •

You can use visualisation techniques to practice. Close your eyes and take the time to experience the situation you are about to face. Let emotions, thoughts and sensations come to you... The brain confuses reality with the imaginary, so training by visualising the situation is equivalent to actually living it. Now you have a technique for training. Through visualisation, you can train yourself to live any situation.

• • •

"First you must dare, then you must dose."

KARINE VIARD

• • •

When you are called upon to dare, remember when you learned to walk. You were very small. You were fragile and yet you dared to stand up. Why did you dare? Because you had no doubt that you were going to succeed. You were going to fall, you were going to cry, you were going to get bumps and maybe even scratch your knee, but you were going to make it. Be aware – you can do anything, nothing is impossible! Focus on this idea and you'll succeed in everything you do because you can do it.

• • •

Yes we can!

BARAK OBAMA

• • •

The world is divided into three lands:

"The land of comfort"

In this land, you master everything, you are perfectly at ease. You know the people and things in this land well, you are used to interacting with them. It's easy to be self-confident in this land, but it's also sclerotic and boring.

"The land of challenge"

When you enter this land, you no longer control everything. There are many new things and new people. You must draw on your resources to adapt to this newness. Entering the land of challenge is both unsettling and terribly exciting.

"The land of danger"

In this land, you don't master anything, or at least not much. So it's potentially dangerous. If you venture into the land of danger, you'll have to learn and adapt at high speed. You'll live at high speed, but you must hang on!

Learn how to regularly escape the land of comfort. Venture into the land of challenge and your territory will become larger and larger. This means that the older you get, the freer you'll be. And if you explore all the lands, eventually at the end of your life, you'll no longer be afraid of anything; you'll have absolute confidence in yourself. Then you'll be able to enter the last land without hesitation. And at the moment of your death you'll be as you are when enjoying a coffee in the sun.

• • •

"Self-confidence is a permanent victory over the unpredictability of life; it is not acquired outright, but it must be recharged, rebuilt, confirmed and embellished every day, to be able to face both the movement of existence and the irruption of the unacceptable."

JACQUES SALOMÉ

• • •

I know you well now and what I can tell you is that I trust you. I know I can count on you. I know your qualities, your talents, your advantages... If you need, ask me and I'll tell you all the great things I think about you. My words will be like a great bowl of energy for you to drink – they will recharge your batteries and help you overcome the obstacles that await you on the path of life. I'm here to help you. We're here. We trust you.

"No..."

IN THE EARLY DAYS OF OUR FRIENDSHIP, I NOTICED THAT YOU VERY OFTEN SAID "NO" TO A LOT OF THINGS.

THIS IS WHAT I'D HAVE LIKED TO TELL YOU...
IF I'D FOUND THE WORDS TO OPEN YOUR HEART AND GET YOU TO SAY "YES"...

...I WOULD PROBABLY HAVE STARTED BY TELLING YOU THE STORY OF "NO MAN".

Once upon a time there was a man who led a normal life in which not much happened. He was a banker. Like many people, he had divorced his wife, with whom he had not had any children, as he had never wanted them. Every day of his life was similar to the previous one and he knew it would be similar to the next. When his friends suggested something new, he always said "No". When the manager of his company offered him the opportunity to change jobs, he would always say "No". When a client came to ask for a loan, he almost always said "No". In fact he almost always said "No" to everything.

One day, as he was walking down the street, he saw an old friend coming towards him. To escape this encounter – meeting old friends bored him – he rushed into an alley and went into a large building to hide. What he didn't know was that inside this building there lived a great marabout. When the marabout saw him, he immediately understood that he was suffering from the

"No" disease. So, without the man realising it, he cast a spell on him so that he would be forced to say "Yes" to every suggestion made to him. This very powerful spell would prevent him from uttering two words: "No" and "But...".

When he left the building, the man met a beggar who asked him for money. Of course he wanted to say "No" as he normally did, but when he wanted to say the word, no sound came out of his mouth. He could only say "Yes" so he was forced to take out his wallet and give the beggar his money. A woman passing by on the street at that moment called him and said: "that's a really nice thing you're doing". She gave him a smile and a look that immediately pleased him. For she was a very beautiful woman. She asked him to come and help the poor the next day. Again he wanted to say "No", but he couldn't.

On his way home, he received a call from a friend who asked him to come and party. It was Wednesday and the man wasn't used to going out during the week – he preferred to rest so he was fit for work. After all, it took a lot of energy to say "No" to all his clients. This time he couldn't do it. He had to say "Yes". The rest of the evening was totally insane. He accepted all the drinks that were offered to him and once he was drunk he did all the stupid things that his friends suggested, so he ended up doing all sorts of things... He woke up the next day with a big headache, but he couldn't deny that he had had an absolutely memorable evening.

He was very tired, but as he'd promised to go and help the poor, he went to the association where the woman had invited him. In the meantime, he said "Yes" to his clients' loan requests, from the most reasonable to the most eccentric. In the evening, he worked for several hours distributing warm clothes and food to homeless people. It was an extraordinary experience for him because he had forgotten the meaning of the word "GIVE". The woman, who seemed very attracted to him, invited him to dinner the following weekend and even though he felt like saying "No" because he was afraid of having his heart broken, he could only say "YES". And that's how his week went...

A few months later he married the woman he had met. She was a very beautiful person, really nice and pleasant and he had eventually fallen in love with her. One evening, as he was crossing the road without looking, a man shouted "LOOK OUT" and pushed him onto the pavement – thanks to his actions, he narrowly avoided a bus that was speeding down the boulevard. The man who had just saved him was none other than the beggar to whom he had given all his money a few months earlier. That day he bought the newspaper and read an article about an inventor whose start-up was worth several million dollars. He recognised one of his wacky clients to whom he had lent a large sum of money.

By saying "YES" to life, he had changed the world*!

• • •

By learning to say "YES", you learn to open up possibilities, to create opportunities for happiness. By saying "YES", you call upon the healing power of life. In fairy tales, all heroes have a good fairy who watches over them. Well, when you say YES, you call upon your good fairy and ask her to take care of you and create wonderful things in your life. All you must do is believe in yourself, in others and in the world and every door will open.

• • •

Life is like a bedroom. In this room, there is a window overlooking a pretty meadow with a horse in it. You have the choice between watching the show from the warmth of the interior, sheltered

---

* This story is loosely based on the film: *Yes Man* (2008).

from the wind, sun and rain, or you can open the window.... You can open the window and take a deep breath and feel the fresh air penetrate deep inside you and pushing back on all the limits that are inside your being. And then feel the freedom...

Carried by this new energy, you can climb through this window, go up on the roof and climb down the drainpipe... You can pick a flower and twirl with your arms spread out like a child playing... And you can also go to this meadow – you can run after the horse and even climb on its back, and with a light tap of your heel you can tell it to gallop! Where will you go? Nobody knows, not even you. But everything you see, hear and feel gives you a taste for adventure.

• • •

Life is an adventure. Life constantly has something to offer you and you have the choice between saying "YES" or "NO". If you say "YES", then you make the choice of discovery, novelty, encounter... if you say "NO" you make the choice of control, protection and withdrawal. Life is like a torrent of living water. To say "NO" is to try to build a dam on a hill to hold back the flowing water. To say "YES" is to get on a raft and let yourself be carried away by the current.

• • •

"The answer is yes. But what was the question?"

WOODY ALLEN

• • •

Fortune favours the brave. To say "YES" is to let yourself be carried away by the whirlwind of life... Every time you say "NO", you erect a wall. Every time you say "NO", you create a blockage. Learn how to remove this word from your vocabulary. Replace it with "YES" and replace it with "YES, BUT..." if you want to make certain conditions. You'll see how this attitude will free the energies around you, how your family and friends will allow themselves to suggest new things.

• • •

Did you know that in China, we never say "NO"? To say "NO" is to lose face, in other words to be ashamed of yourself in front of your peers. Since we are not allowed to say "NO", we express our disagreement, by implication, to influence the request made to us. In this way, without creating confrontations that would mean one of the two parties losing face, one reaches a consensus, which preserves harmony in human relations.

• • •

Every time you say "NO", ask yourself. Ask yourself why you tried to go against your destiny. Was it because you didn't want to? Was it because you were afraid? Was it "NO" was your mechanical answer? In your mind, there are probably fears and beliefs that prevent you from freeing yourself, from letting go. You probably want to control everything so that nothing bad happens in your life. You don't want to take any risks.

• • •

"The child cannot learn to walk if he refuses to fall. "

ANONYMOUS

• • •

A group of students are studying the Seven Wonders of the World in Geography class. The teacher asks the students to make a list of the Seven Wonders of the World. With a few exceptions, the students write the following answers on their sheet:

1 – The Pyramids of Egypt
2 – The Great Wall of China
3 – The Taj Mahal in India
4 – The Easter Island statues
5 – The pyramids of Chichén Itza in Mexico
6 – The Colosseum of Rome
7 – The Alhambra in Spain

While listening to the answers, the teacher sees a calm young girl who has not yet begun to write her answer. He then asks her if she is having any problems with the list.

The girl replies: "Yes, I must admit that I can't make up my mind. There are so many of them..."
Intrigued, the teacher asks her: "Tell me what you're thinking about and I might be able to help you."
The girl hesitates, then starts to write:

1 – Seeing
2 – Hearing
3 – Touching
4 – Feeling...

She still hesitates and then continues with her list:

5 – Running
6 – Laughter
7 – Love

• • •

So what are your seven wonders of the world? What would you like to do? What trip, what project, what discovery, what pleasure do you definitely want to say "YES" to without worrying about "what will people say", social conventions or some silly rule learned by rote at school or in a bygone era. Be free at last! And if you are free, you'll have the power to say "YES". And if you say "YES" life will smile on you like a wondrous sun.

Seeing yourself grow old

I KNOW THAT THINKING ABOUT OLD AGE WORRIES YOU
AND MAKES YOU SAD. BUT IF YOU WILL LET ME,
I'D LIKE TO SHARE MY VIEWS ON THIS SUBJECT

LET ME SHOW YOU HOW AGING IS ACTUALLY
AN OPPORTUNITY THAT LIFE OFFERS US, A GIFT THAT
WE MUST KNOW HOW TO WELCOME BECAUSE IT BRINGS
SO MANY BENEFITS...

...LET ME TELL YOU THIS AMAZING STORY.

One stormy evening, a woman lying on her deathbed asks her niece to read the newspaper aloud to her. Eighty years earlier, a little boy had been born with the appearance and body of an old man. The little boy's mother died after giving birth and the father abandoned the child on a church square. A couple found the child and decided to take him in and raise him as their own son.

The little boy does not learn to walk until he is nine years old. At the beginning of his life he can only use a wheelchair, then he walks on crutches. His face is very strange because it is terribly wrinkled. His bones are as brittle as those of an old man. The little boy seems to be suffering from a serious illness. He has the face of a centenarian, but strangely every year that passes seems to make him a year younger.

As a teenager, the young boy falls in love with a young girl. The girl is both frightened and intrigued by this strange-looking boy. Nothing happens between them. But several years later, he finds himself on the platform of a train station. The girl has become a beautiful young woman. She is surprised to see the young boy again, who has changed a lot. Now he seems to be in his sixties.

They leave each other on the station platform, but ten years later, they meet again by chance. This time they are the same age, forty. They fall in love and have a passionate romance before getting married and having two children. Time goes by. The woman gets older and the man gets younger – now she is almost fifty years old, while he seems to be no more than thirty. The young man gets scared and runs away.

She does not find him again until a few years later. When she is almost seventy, she meets him in a park while riding her bike. The man who is still her husband and the father of her two children is now only ten years old. He has the maturity of a man, but the face of a pre-teenager. Time separates them for good. She is old enough to be his grandmother. This meeting is like a rip in time.

She decides to welcome him into her home and take care of him. The years go by and the boy keeps getting younger and younger until he becomes an infant who pees in his pants. She takes care of him as she herself grows older. By the time she reaches 85, the boy is the age of an infant. As she holds him in her arms, the little angel stops breathing and dies. Thus ends the life of the love of her life*.

• • •

* Story loosely based on the film: *The Strange Story of Benjamin Button* (2008)

This amazing story can make you wonder about the passage of time and the meaning of life. Sometimes you may despair of growing old, but what would happen if life were the other way around? You would be born an old man and end your life as a new-born baby. Would that be better? The passage of time transforms, brings you closer or further away. The passage of time turns us into the children that we are, into full-fledged adults before turning us into hobbling, spoiled old men. Isn't that a good thing?

• • •

Did you know that in Japan, old people are highly respected? They are respected as sacred figures. One day while I was walking through the streets of Tokyo, I even saw a statue of an elderly lady. She was a benefactor who had done a lot for the poor and orphans of Tokyo. It was very strange for me to see this statue, because in the West all statues have smooth skin, big muscles and chubby faces. Yet one can be admired in old age.

• • •

A famous* biologist said, "we don't know whether man is a flower or a chair." For this biologist, the chair is eternal from the moment we take care not to damage it and repair it when needed. The flower, in almost the opposite way, already carries the programme of its own end in its genes. It is programmed to die. If Man is a flower, this would mean that it would be possible, by modifying his genetic programme, to allow him to attain immortality.

• • •

---

* Jean Rostand (1894-1977).

Imagine your life if you were immortal. It would mean that you would remain eternally young and have an infinite amount of time ahead of you. After a certain age, you would no longer experience any physical transformation. Only your soul would continue to evolve. You would look like your children. But would people have children? Would they want to? And would it be possible, because there would not be enough room on this earth to accommodate all people? If immortality existed, you would probably never have been born...

. . .

In your life, I'm sure you've climbed a mountain. Maybe it was a very high mountain or maybe it was just a hill, it doesn't matter. Just remember. On the way up you had to do a lot of work because the slope was steep. But every once in a while you could stop to breathe and admire the beautiful landscape, and no doubt you were accompanied by people you loved and with whom you could talk, complain and laugh about this superhuman effort you were making.

And when you reached the top of the mountain, then what beauty! You could see the landscape all around you and it was breath-taking. You could enjoy both the beauty of the landscape and the pleasure of being able to let your muscles rest at last. And all the people who had made the journey were so happy and satisfied with the journey and the day. There was an atmosphere of joy and a deep sense of accomplishment among the whole little troop of walkers.

Growing old is not so different from climbing a mountain. Life is a succession of efforts and moments of rest, encounters, difficult moments and moments of joy. Growing old is just taking a path and moving forward to discover new sensations, new landscapes. Growing old means growing up. It's like climbing a mountain. And when you get to the top, at the end of your life: wow, you can contemplate everything you've done. You have a mountain of memories to tell and to remember! You're at peace.

The advantage of old age over hiking is that once you've reached the top, you don't have to come back down...

• • •

"To protest against the passing of time, the old men fast."

LES NULS

• • •

One day, the king's jester became too insolent. The king, who was extremely strict with his subjects, said to him:
"My dear fool, you are too insolent, I condemn you to death... But as you have often made me laugh, I grant you the right to choose how you die. Tell me what you want to die, and I will grant your choice."

What does the jester choose to avoid death?

The jester replied: "I choose to die of old age!"

• • •

Old age is an opportunity. The more time passes, the older the body gets and the more the soul and spirit grow. Every day that passes is a year of gaining experience, knowledge and wisdom. Growing older means growing – be happy to grow older because each year that passes makes you wiser and more spiritual. Every year that passes makes you better. So you get better and more valuable every day. And in the end, when you are at your best, you can be proud of how far you've come.

. . .

There are Men who are called the Men Without Sons. These men do not accept the passage of time. They want to remain in the forefront, to dominate others. They only think of their own interests. These men have no sons because they refuse to teach and pass on their knowledge to the youngest. They don't want to share their power because they want to keep their place forever. I've seen these men suffer terribly as they approach old age because there is nothing left after them.

. . .

Follow the natural movement of life. Learn when you're young, do when you're an adult and pass on when you're old. In this way you'll take your rightful place, and by taking your rightful place you'll live in harmony with the world around you. Every time has its pleasures – learning is a joy, doing is a joy, passing on knowledge is a joy. Happiness, remember, is the result of a decision. Whether you are young, mature or old, you'll be happy if you have decided to be, and if this decision is irrevocable.

. . .

"You start getting older when you finish learning."

JAPANESE PROVERB

. . .

According to an ancient legend, there is a fountain of youth, which allows those who bathe in it to regain their youth. If you want to live old and healthy, you too must find your fountain of youth. Is it a passion that drives you, is it a game that takes you back to your youth, is it love that makes your heart beat and your soul vibrate? Find your fountain of youth – whether it's a place, a person, a book, a music, a dish or an activity. Find it and go there as often as you can.

• • •

"Youth is not entirely a time of life,
it is a state of mind. It is a temper of the will,
a quality of the imagination,
a vigour of the emotions,
a temperamental predominance of courage over timidity,
an appetite for adventure over love of ease.
Nobody grows old by merely living a number of years;
People grow old only by deserting their ideals.
Years may wrinkle the skin, but to give up interest wrinkles the soul.
Worry, doubt, self-distrust, fear and despair –
these are the long, long years that bow the head
and turn the growing spirit back to dust.
Whatever your years, there is in every being's
heart the love of wonder, the undaunted challenge
of events, the unfailing child-like appetite for
what next, and the joy in the game of life.
You are as young as your faith, as old as your doubt;
as young as your self-confidence, as old as your fear;
as young as your hope, as old as your despair.
In the central place of every heart there is a
recording chamber; so long as it receives messages
of beauty, hope, cheer and courage, so long are you young.
When the wires are all down and your heart is covered
with the moss of pessimism and the ice of cynicism,
then, and then only, are you grown old."

GENERAL MAC ARTHUR

• • •

Just as happiness is the result of a decision, youth is the result of a decision. I know physically older men and women who have more energy and drive than twenty-year-olds. I share General MacArthur's conviction. Charm and beauty are built more than they are inherited. Haven't you ever met men or women whose beauty has grown with age? This is a fact that cannot be denied. So build.

• • •

"Fear of getting old is more damaging than age."

JEANNE MOREAU

• • •

I love the very old
sitting at the window
who look on with a smile
at the cloudy sky
and the light that limps in the streets of winter

I love their faces
with a thousand wrinkles
which are the memory of a thousand lives
that make a man's life

I like the very old hand
that caresses while shaking
the child's forehead
like the leaning tree
brushes its branches
the clarity of a river

I like in old people
their fragile and slow gesture

that holds every moment of life
like a porcelain cup

as we should do ourselves
at any time
with life

JEAN-PIERRE SIMÉON
IN PRAISE OF OLD AGE

• • •

We will grow old together. We share this common destiny. So let's try to accept it and make the best of it. Let us be an example for our children so that they have confidence in the future. Let us be happy with this movement as the water flows down the slope, let us be proud of the efforts made, the challenges taken up and the tasks duly accomplished. Every day, our memory fills up a little more with memories that are like treasures we dare to offer.

• • •

Only yesterday, I was twenty years old
I caressed time, I enjoyed life
Like one savours love
And I lived for the night
Without counting my days
That were wasting away with time
I've made so many plans that never came to life
I've built on so many hopes that withered away
I will stay lost, not knowing where to go
The eyes are searching the sky
But the heart is tied to the ground
Yesterday, when I was young
The taste of life was sweet as rain upon my tongue

I teased at life as if it were a foolish game
The way the evening breeze may tease a candle flame
The thousand dreams I dreamed, the splendid things I planned
I always built, alas, on weak and shifting sand
I lived by night and shunned the naked light of day
And only now I see the years ran away
The game of love I played with arrogance and pride
And every flame I lit too quickly, quickly died
The friends I made all seemed somehow to drift away
And only I am left on stage to end the play
There are so many songs in me that won't be sung
I feel the bitter taste of tears upon my tongue
The time has come for me to pay for yesterday
When I was young

CHARLES AZNAVOUR,
YESTERDAY, WHEN I WAS YOUNG, 1964

Separating

WHEN I SAW YOU, YOU'D JUST SEPARATED FROM
SOMEONE WHO'D BEEN IMPORTANT IN YOUR LIFE...
YOU WERE SAD AND DISTRAUGHT...

THIS IS WHAT I'D HAVE LIKED TO TELL YOU...
IF I'D HAD MORE TIME TO DISCUSS THIS SEPARATION...

...I WOULD PROBABLY HAVE STARTED BY TELLING YOU
THIS STORY...

Once upon a time there was a child who had not yet been born. He loved his mother so much that at the moment of delivery he prayed to God to let him live in her womb. This is what he said:

"God, I don't want to part with my mother. I love her. I feel what she feels. I eat what she eats. I drink what she drinks. I'd like you to grant me the right to live in her womb, bound to her forever."

God, moved by the child's entreaties, laughs heartily.
"You are afraid of separating," he says, "and you want to live your whole life in her womb."
"Yes, I do!" repeated the child.
"Then your wish is granted." conceded God.
The child savoured his victory and thus continued to live in the womb. But nature ensured that he continued to grow. His arms, head and legs continued to grow while the amniotic fluid pouch that sheltered him did not. At first, he was happy to bend in

half and tighten himself up. But soon the situation became untenable. He was squeezed together like a can of sardines. He wanted to get out, but the passage had become too narrow. Meanwhile, his mother was suffering terrible stomach pains.

Without the help of a doctor, who saved them both with an operation, the child and the mother would have died.

Several years later, the child who had become an adult remembered this moment. "To separate is to live!" he whispered as he served his mother a cup of tea and continued to visit her every day of his life.

• • •

"Life begins with a separation and an encounter."

ANONYMOUS

• • •

Today you must face a separation. Someone you love has moved away far away, and it's hard to bear. It hurts you and I understand. I too have experienced painful separations. I know how much it hurts. If you agree, I can help you understand what's going on inside you. By understanding it better, you'll discover a new way of looking at things. And maybe you'll give this separation a new meaning.

• • •

A separation is the result of a growth of your inner being. This is exactly what happens when a child is born and becomes an adult. Each time, you grow inside and transform into a new being. To become this new being, you must separate yourself from certain places, certain habits, certain people. All your life, if you let your inner being grow, you'll have to separate. Each separation will mean that you are growing and rising.

· · ·

Once upon a time there were three acorns. These three acorns were threads of the same branch of the same oak tree. They had also fallen on the same spot. Being perennial, as soon as it rained, they had germinated and buried their roots deep in the ground. Three young shoots and then three shrubs appeared in the clearing next to the great oak, the father of all acorns. The three shrubs were almost the same, with one difference. One of them was half a centimetre taller.

The three shrubs grew in the shelter of the large oak tree. At first, nobody paid too much attention to this half-centimetre difference. However, because of its size, the largest of the three shrubs received more light than its two brothers and therefore grew faster. In the beginning it was not so visible, but after three years it was thirty centimetres taller and after ten years it was more than two metres taller, so that its leaves began to hide the light from its brothers.

The more time passed, the more light it received and the less light its brothers received. It felt sorry for them but continued to grow further and further away without being able to do anything, its deepest nature was to grow and to go higher and higher in search of light. After a few years, its two brothers began to decline. Deprived of light, they were unable to draw enough strength. They became more fragile and racked by diseases and animals, so that one winter they died.

The great oak was very sad but had to face the facts. That was life! It was one of the few acorns that reached the state of an oak tree. Now it had to play its role in the forest. Birds had nested in its branches. In the summer it provided shade for walkers. It protected plants and trees from the wind and many species lived at its feet. It had to follow its destiny. The separation was not sad, and neither was death, just the result of life, which is growth and death.

"Living is torture because living separates."

ALBERT CAMUS

Every time you part from someone, be happy, because it means you are growing up. The day you separate from your parents is the day you become an adult, an independent and free being. The day you separate from a friend is the day you choose your path and become someone. The day you separate from your spouse is the day on the path of life when you have taken different roads, and to be yourself you have decided to live apart. Separation is the fruit of the desire to be yourself.

Life is a period of long uninterrupted growth. When young, physical growth dominates. As an adult, it is psychological growth. In between, human beings grow. Their ego asserts itself, frees itself from conventions, expresses its expectations and needs, learns to say no. This growth is made of liberations and ruptures. Each break-up means that you can be a little more yourself. Those who never break up are those who remain prisoners of their past and of a settled identity.

"The job of parents is to know how to separate themselves from their children."

MARCEL RUFO

The important thing when two people separate is to avoid hurting each other. It is rare for the two beings to be aware that they are in fact in full transformation and that the break-up is necessary. Very often, they take the separation as a rejection, a lack of love or contempt, but this is not the case. If one separates, it is because it is necessary for one's own happiness and fulfilment. When you hurt each other, it is because one is unable to realise that you can no longer live together.

• • •

"An encounter is only the beginning of a separation."

JAPANESE PROVERB

• • •

In friendship, separations are never more than temporary. At certain times, we are very close and then we become very far away and then we get closer again. Sometimes we lose sight of each other for several months or years and then we find each other and rediscover each other. We return renewed, enriched by our experiences, happy to be able to share and tell them. We have a big party, we often drink more than we should, we remember the past and then we say goodbye again and see you soon?

• • •

... Let's drink one last time
To friendship, love and joy
We did celebrate our reunion
But now I have to go, even though it makes me sad...

GRAEME ALLWRIGHT, IL FAUT QUE JE M'EN AILLE, 1966

• • •

In love, separation is a promise. Separation stokes the fire of passion. O what a feeling to kiss your lips on the platform of a train station or when getting off the plane, to finally be able to hug each other, to touch your skin, to feel your warmth, to kiss your cheeks, to look at your eyes, to make love all night long drunk with joy and the happiness of finding each other again after those days as long as an eternity... These are unique, intense, orgasmic sensations... that we pay the price of separation.

• • •

"To meet again after a long separation is more pleasant than a wedding night."

CHINESE PROVERB

• • •

There is also the separation of couples who have loved each other, which is often painful at least for one of the two partners, still in love, still attached, while the other one leaves... For the one who is still in love, this wound will have to be healed. If this is your case, you have the right to be sad and to cry. You have the right to listen to songs that remind you of the past and to wallow in nostalgia. And when you've had your fill, get up and live, because life is strong in you.

• • •

We've often seen
Fire flowing again
From an ancient volcano
Considered too old
It's said that there are
Fire-scorched lands
That yield more wheat
Than the best April
And when evening comes
With a burning sky
The red and the black--
Are they not joined together?
Don't leave me
Don't leave me
Don't leave me
Don't leave me

JACQUES BREL, NE ME QUITTE PAS, 1966

• • •

And then there is separation from one's family. When the children grow up and leave the house that had been full of laughter and arguments, leaving the place a little empty and silent... Let's be happy to see them take flight, become fulfilled men and women and take advantage of this to live a second youth... see past loves or friends again, meet new people and live new adventures. Let the children take flight and take flight yourself once more!

• • •

Dear parents, I leave
I love you, but I leave
You won't have children anymore, tonight
I'm not fleeing, I fly
Understand well, I fly
Without any smoke, without any alcohol I fly, I fly

I really thought my mother was suspecting something
She asked me if I was sick
Why I was so pale,

I said I was fine,
It's really clear, I think she has pretended to believe me
And my father has smiled.

Oh, above all don't turn back, get away a little more
There is the station,
And after the station, there is the Atlantic Ocean,

Dear parents, I leave
I love you, but I leave
You won't have children anymore, tonight
I'm not fleeing, I fly
Understand well, I fly
Without any smoke, without any alcohol I fly, I fly

MICHEL SARDOU, JE VOLE, 1978

Making an important decision

WHEN I SAW YOU, YOU HAD TO MAKE
AN IMPORTANT DECISION... YOU WERE AFRAID
OF MAKING THE WRONG ONE.

THIS IS WHAT I'D HAVE LIKED TO TELL YOU...
TO GIVE YOU THE MEANS TO MAKE THE RIGHT DECISION...

...I WOULD PROBABLY HAVE STARTED BY TELLING YOU
THIS STORY.

A young couple had just decided to move into a new flat. They had bought a flat in a brand-new residence consisting of twelve identical flats with balconies. They invested all their money in this purchase. Also, when it came to decorating, they had rather limited means. They nevertheless decided to wallpaper the walls of their living room.

Being inexperienced in the field of decoration and interior design, they decide to ask their neighbour, who had also decided to wallpaper, for advice: "Hello! We've noticed that you've just been papering your apartment. We were planning on doing the same – how many rolls did you buy?" "Nine," replies the neighbour!

The next day, the young couple goes to a DIY shop and buys nine rolls of wallpaper. They spend their whole weekend hanging it but once they've finished, they find that they still have four full rolls left. They're a bit disappointed because they've wasted money on the spare rolls and angry with their neighbour for giving them the wrong information.

The next day, they pass him in the lift. "Hello, you told us you'd bought nine rolls of wallpaper for your living room. We took your advice and bought nine as well, but we still have four left! "And the neighbour replies: "Oh, you too!*"

. . .

When you want to make a decision, especially an important one, don't rely on the opinions of others, who might not have the same approach to life as you. They don't have the same expectations or the same personality. Also, their advice is likely to reflect more what they would do if they were in your shoes than what you should do. By following their advice, you may make a decision that would be good for them, but not for you.

If you are planning a trip to a country and ask someone what to visit, chances are they'll advise you to go to a museum if they like museums, to go on a nature hike if they like nature hikes, and to visit a monument if they like history. The advice people give you is just a reflection of what they like or dislike. Their advice tells you more about them than it does about the right decision for you.

. . .

Once upon a time there was a woman who was born on an island. Her mother was a cantankerous woman who drank copious amounts of alcohol, while her sisters were illiterate and spent their time doing stupid things. She was the only one who was serious and worked at school.

---

* This story is taken from the book: *Manager, a real game with NLP* (2002).

Throughout her life, she took care of her mother and sisters for whom she felt responsible. She was afraid that something would happen to them, so she spent all her time and money helping her mother and sisters, even though they were behaving badly.

She was unhappy because she had a good job and made a good living, but she had never been able to do what she really liked. So, one day she went to see a psychologist for help.

After he had listened to her tale, he opened one of the drawers of his desk and pulled out two small iron devices that were actually compasses. He put them on her desk so that she could see them clearly. And he told her:

"The needle of the first compass always points towards 'self-sacrifice'. If you follow this needle, you'll always do what it takes to be "normal", to respect social conventions and to assume the role that others want you to play.

The needle of the second compass always points to "happiness". If you follow this needle, you'll always do everything to have a life in accordance with your true inner self.

Which compass do you want to follow now?"

Which compass do you think this woman chose to follow?

She chooses to follow the compass of social conventions. She was too afraid of being judged and considered a bad mother because she did not take good care of her son, of being a bad daughter because she did not take good care of her mother and of being a bad sister because she did not help her sisters. Yet none of these three people ever did her any good or brought her happiness.

If she had chosen the compass of happiness, she would have become an example to her son, her mother and her sisters, an example of someone who is successful in life. She would have made them see their own responsibilities. Because everyone, even children, is the master of their own lives. It is up to each person to make decisions, to choose their models, to take a path. We are not responsible for what happens to others. We have no power over their lives, even over the lives of our children.

• • •

Which compass do you want to follow? Do you want to follow the compass of social conventions and be a "normal" person or do you want to drop the mask and be yourself? Are you willing to pay the price? The price of questioning your entitlements, your status, your value in society. Following the compass of happiness means following a new way of assessing your life, no longer according to your success and status but according to your well-being and personal fulfilment.

• • •

When faced with an important decision to make, remember the answer you have already given to these four questions:

- What are my values?
- What are my needs?
- What is my deepest personality?
- What are my talents?

Always choose the decision that is closest to your values, that will enable you to meet your needs, that will be in line with your deepest personality and that will allow you to make use of your talents. To make good decisions, you must first get to know yourself well.

• • •

"Have the courage to follow your heart and intuition.
They somehow already know what you truly want to become.
Everything else is secondary."

STEVE JOBS, SPEECH AT STANFORD IN 2005

• • •

The thing that can most help you make the right decisions is your intuition. Intuition is a perception that is not rational or based on logic. Intuition is the intelligence of the heart. When you start thinking, your unconscious has already analysed all the parameters of the situation and has already made its decision known to you in the form of intuition. Your unconscious mind is always thinking about how to protect you and bring you the best in your life, so listen to it!

• • •

"Intuition is a view from the heart in the darkness."

ANDRÉ SUARÈS

• • •

"It is with logic that we prove and with intuition that we find."

HENRI POINCARÉ

• • •

It's impossible to know all the consequences of your decisions. Fate is impenetrable. You may think that a decision will have positive consequences, yet the reverse is true. The only thing you can be sure of is your ability to make sure the decision you make is the right one. Make your decision quickly and then take action to make sure it's the right one. That's how the decision you make will actually become the right decision.

• • •

"When someone makes a decision, he is really diving into a strong current that will carry him to places he had never dreamed of when he first made the decision."

PAULO COELHO, THE ALCHEMIST

Suffering from bad luck

WHEN I GOT HOME I THOUGHT ABOUT WHAT
WE'D SAID TO EACH OTHER...AND I WANT YOU TO KNOW
THAT I UNDERSTAND YOU....

YOU'VE HAD SO MUCH BAD LUCK THAT YOU THINK YOU
ARE "CURSED"?

AT THE TIME, I COULDN'T FIND THE WORDS TO EASE
YOUR MIND... BUT HERE'S WHAT I'D HAVE LIKED
TO SAY TO SHOW YOU THAT THINGS ARE NOT ALWAYS
AS THEY SEEM...

AND I WOULD PROBABLY HAVE STARTED BY TELLING YOU
THIS AMAZING STORY.

A boat was shipwrecked on a reef in the middle of the ocean. The only survivor had managed to swim to a small, deserted island far away from the shipping lanes. Every day he prayed for someone to come and save him. He would sit on the highest rock on the island and spend his day watching the horizon. But he never saw any ships passing by.

To protect himself from the strong sun during the day and the cold at night, he made a small hut out of branches. He was immensely proud of his hut because it was solid and provided shelter and gave him the feeling that he had a home on this island populated only by wild animals.

Just a few days later, on his way back from a day's hunt, he saw smoke. It was his hut that was burning – the sun had been beating through the broken glass of a bottle all day long and had set the dried palm branches on fire. The man fell to his knees in desperation.

He wept until he was out of tears, spending the night lamenting his fate and wondering why he was so unlucky. Being shipwrecked was not enough, he also had to lose his cabin and the only things he had managed to save from the wreck, and which he had counted on to survive, in a fire.

Exhausted with sorrow, anger, groggy from the cold of the night, he ended up falling asleep on the beach. Early the next morning, he was woken up by a foghorn. He rubbed his eyes and saw, as in a dream, the silhouette of a boat anchored offshore and a rowboat being thrown into the sea.

When he was on the ship, he asked the captain: "How did you know I was here?" The astonished captain replied: "But we saw your smoke signals*!"

• • •

An old horse breeder owned a beautiful mare which she used to plough her fields. One day the mare disappeared. She had escaped from her paddock during the night. All the people of came to her in pity. But she answered them: "Is it good or bad luck? I couldn't say."

Seven days later, the mare reappeared, followed by a magnificent stallion who would give her beautiful foals – she'd be able to start breeding again and earn some money. The people of the

---

* Story adapted freely from: *For the heart and for the mind* (2011).

village came to see her to congratulate her. But she replied: "Is it good or bad luck? I couldn't say."

The breeder's son tried to ride the stallion and train him. But he was a particularly wild stallion and in doing so he had a bad fall and broke his leg. All the people of the village came to her in pity. Again, she said, "Is it good or bad luck? I couldn't say."

A month later, a conscription agent came to the village. Their country had just gone to war and all young men in good health were being conscripted to go to the front. Because of his broken leg, the farmer's son could not be conscripted and did not go to war.

The woman then says to herself: "Is it good or bad luck? I can't say."

. . .

It is human nature to evaluate the events that occur in one's daily life. But we lack the power to predict or control everything. Faced with the hazards of life, we should beware of drawing hasty conclusions. Over time, our vision becomes more refined, our judgement becomes more precise, new elements may come into play and contradict our first impressions. This is how certain events can seem to herald insurmountable difficulties, whereas they are undoubtedly opportunities.

. . .

Do you know the law of buttered toast? This law is a variant of Murphy's Law, which states that "anything that can go wrong will go wrong". In short, it means that when something bad can happen, it happens. Applied to a buttered slice of bread, it means that if you drop your slice, it will always fall on the buttered side… leaving a nasty greasy stain on your floor and your slice dirty with dust, only good for the bin…

In fact, this law is wrong. It has been studied by experts who have shown that out of 300 "buttered slices", the slice of bread falls 148 times on the buttered side and 152 times on the non-buttered side. Whether or not the slice of bread falls on the buttered side actually depends on a range of parameters, including the height of the table which, depending on the conditions, allows it to make a half or full turn. And how annoying it is also depends on the cleanliness of the floor in question…

Murphy's Law is itself linked to the LMA or "law of maximum annoyance". According to this law, when something goes wrong, something worse always happens at the same time. In short, be careful. If you drop your buttered toast – it may fall on its buttered side and in a moment of inattention your foot slips on the butter left on the floor, causing you to tip over backwards and break your leg. Fortunately, intelligence can prevent this kind of annoyance.

• • •

Luck or misfortune are not related only to chance. In fact, they mainly depend on your attitudes. For example, people who are always in conflict with other people are often angry, proud and uncompromising. They complain of meeting conflicts every day that they actually help create. They therefore create their own bad luck. By changing their attitudes, they can therefore bring luck back into their relationships.

• • •

"The definition of insanity is doing the same thing over and over again and expecting different results."

ALBERT EINSTEIN

• • •

If you repeatedly encounter the same types of events and think you are constantly unlucky, ask yourself how you make your choices and act. Maybe you make bad choices by following bad scenarios that always bring the same problems. This often happens in love or in the professional field. The same causes produce the same effects, so by changing the causes, you can also change the consequences and bring luck back into your life!

• • •

"The life we have today is, whether we like it or not, the product of all the choices we have made, or refused to make!"

PHILIPPE GABILLIET

• • •

"I have always trusted premonitory dreams," says an inveterate gambler. "One day in a dream I saw a thoroughbred whose jockey was wearing the number 7 on his helmet.
When I woke up, I saw that it was exactly 7:07 a.m. and that it was the 7th day of the month.
While reading the newspaper I discovered that in the seventh race a horse called "Seven Dwarves" was to run. I withdrew all my money and bet 7,000 euros on it.
– Oh right, and he finished first?
– No. Seventh..."

• • •

If you think you're unlucky, read these seven true stories:

In December 2012, in a Spanish village called Sodeto, all the inhabitants played the same lottery number on Christmas Eve and won 900 million euros between them. All the inhabitants became rich, all but one, Costis Mitsotakis. He had been forgotten by the organisers of the operation and had therefore not bought a ticket.

On 6 August 1945, Tsutomu Yamaguchi was on his way to Hiroshima. While he was on the tram, the first atomic bomb exploded. He lost part of his hearing and sight. He then went back home to Nagasaki. In Nagasaki, the second atomic bomb exploded. Tsutomu Yamaguchi thus survived two atomic bombs. He died in 2010 at the age of 93.

Roy Sullivan is a forest ranger who was struck 7 times by lightning between 1942 and 1977. He survived each time.

Erik Norrie attracts bad luck. He was attacked by a shark and lost part of his leg. Before that he had already been struck by lightning, bitten by a poisonous snake, and attacked by monkeys.

Selak is a Croatian teacher. In 1962, he survived the derailment of a train that plunged into a river. Then, a few years later, the plane he was on from Croatia crashed, leaving nineteen people dead except him. Three years later, the bus he was on crashed into a river, killing four people. In 1970, his car exploded after an accident, but he managed to escape from the passenger seat just before the explosion. In 1973, another of his cars exploded. He lost his whole scalp, but not his life. Then, in 1993, he fell under the wheels of a bus. He also survived this accident.

Thirty-year-old Ann Hodge, an American living in Alabama, had her home destroyed by a meteorite in 1954. To this day, she is the only person ever to be struck by a meteorite.

In a French village, the villagers used to always play the same lottery numbers together, until one day in 2012, the tobacconist forgot to confirm the numbers. Except that on that day, the numbers came up...

...

"Luck is not what happens to you, but what you do with what happens to you."

RICHARD WISEMAN

...

If something very bad happens to you, you have to ask yourself how you'll react. Ask yourself at least these three questions: Why did this event happen to me? What could I have done to avoid it? What did this event teach me and what could I do to prevent it from happening again in the future? The past has its source in the future... No mistake is serious unless it is repeated and as long as we learn the necessary lessons for the future.

Never burden yourself with chance or bad luck, as this would stop you analysing your own responsibility for what happens to you. Attributing the cause of an event to chance is tantamount to denying responsibility. Whether positive or negative, attributing the occurrence of an event to bad luck or to one's lucky star prevents you from identifying the conduct that leads to failure or success. Failure to identify it prevents oneself from preventing future misfortunes and repeating successes.

...

Are you familiar with creative thinking? Creative thinking means thinking very strongly about a goal or the occurrence of happy events in one's life. By doing so, you prepare yourself to reach this goal and to bring about these events. By mobilising your creative thinking, you promote luck because you unconsciously do what you need to do to make it happen. Dare to imagine a happy future and you will see the end of your troubles.

Adapting to change

WHEN I SAW YOU, YOU WERE FACING A MAJOR CHANGE IN YOUR LIFE... AND YOU WERE STRUGGLING TO AVOID THAT CHANGE...

THIS IS WHAT I'D HAVE LIKED TO TELL YOU... TO HELP YOU MAKE THIS CHANGE AN OPPORTUNITY IN YOUR LIFE...

...I WOULD PROBABLY HAVE STARTED BY TELLING YOU THIS STORY...

Once upon a time there was a drop of water living in the ocean. She liked living there very much – she had a lot of "water drop" friends and everything was going well for her. But one day the temperature started to rise. It was summer and the sun began to heat the surface of the ocean. The drop of water started to feel weird. It was strange, but she felt like she was growing. Yes, it wasn't just an impression, she was growing and growing. And as she grew, she became lighter. All of a sudden, she became so big and so light that she flew away.

She climbed high in the sky and reached a cloud, a foreign place to her, which was filled with drops of water like her that had turned into water vapour. The little drop of water was a little sad because she had left some of her dearest friends in the depths of the ocean, but after a while she made new friends, got used to her new height and weight and began to love her new life in the air, in that cloud which was always flooded with light, either by the sun by day or by the moon by night. It was an incredibly beautiful place.

But one day she felt something else. It suddenly became very cold, and she instantly shrank and became very heavy. And without having time to say "phew", she quickly started to fall… to a place she didn't know, and which was called a mountain. When she fell from the sky, she bounced and landed on a blade of grass. She thought this strange place was her destination, but she started to roll on the grass, fell to the earth and descended to the depths of the earth. She went deeper and deeper before falling into an underground river.

There everything was in chaos. There was a multitude of strange water drops spinning around in all directions at full speed as they went down into the earth. She reappeared in a torrent and continued to descend at full speed down the mountain sides. The next day she descended even further. She was going so fast that she couldn't get her bearings but soon got used to her new life, in which she flowed at speed among thousands of drops of water. Eventually she slowed right down, and she missed the speed. In the end she thought it was a great thing to live in a torrent.

A few weeks later she reached the sea and found the world she had left before. She was surprised to be back to her starting point and told herself that she had probably gone through a natural cycle of transformation. She started a new quiet life with new friends, and everything was going well in the most beautiful ocean, when suddenly she felt the sunlight on her back… She barely had time to think, when suddenly her body became light and big and rose up to the clouds. The great merry-go-round of change had started again, but this time she was no longer afraid!

• • •

The human body is 55% water. This means that it has a huge capacity for change, because water is the medium of change par excellence. It is water on the first day, gas on the second day and ice on the third day. It changes shape according to pressure and temperature, always adapting perfectly to its environment, without ever undergoing any alteration. It adapts to all conditions, changing shape while remaining itself.

When it descends the mountain in the form of a stream and then a torrent, it overcomes obstacles, takes the shortest paths, and adapts to every relief. It doesn't curse the stone that blocks its path, it simply goes around it or, if it can't get through, it seeps into the subsoil to get around it. And if it can't get through, then it overflows. And if it can't overflow, then the sun turns it into steam, and it escapes in a big cloud.

• • •

*"The species that survive are not the strongest,
nor the most intelligent, but those that adapt best to change."*

CHARLES DARWIN

• • •

One day, the cocoon of a butterfly began to crack open. A woman who was watching the scene sat and watched the young butterfly fight long and hard to emerge from its chrysalis, but the woman soon had the feeling that the insect was not going to make it. It seemed exhausted and was barely moving.

Wishing to help, she then grabbed a pair of scissors and delicately cut out the cocoon so the butterfly would find it easier to get out. And indeed, the butterfly emerged easily from the cocoon.

It had a small body with crumpled, atrophied wings. The woman told herself: "It doesn't matter, it will grow".

She opened the window so that the butterfly could fly into the garden when it was ready and went about her business. A few hours later, when she closed the window, she noticed that the butterfly was still there. It hadn't managed to spread its wings and had only managed to walk on the table.

In fact, it never managed to spread its wings. It spent the rest of its life crawling with its small body, unable to use its stunted wings. What the woman had failed to understand when she helped it, was that the cocoon was too narrow and that it was a trick of Nature to force the butterfly to pierce it and to train its wings... Only then can it[*] fly away.

• • •

Every change in your life brings a lot of effort and suffering, which are in fact necessary to help you adapt to the new situation. If you refuse to face reality, then you won't be able to adapt, and instead of gaining the freedom and new possibilities promised by the transformation, you'll lose all your abilities. You'll be neither here nor there, unsuited to the old world that no longer exists and to the new world that is here.

• • •

"When lobsters change shells, they first lose the old one and remain defenceless until they can make a new one. During this time, they are in great danger. For teenagers it's somewhat similar."

FRANÇOISE AND CATHERINE DOLTO

---

* This story is loosely based on an account by Baron D'Olbach (1723-1789).

...

The lobster complex is a symbol of change – every change leads to a moult. During this moult, just as the lobster loses the precious carapace that protects it, men and women are weakened. They no longer know exactly who they are, how to react or how to defend themselves. They are more sensitive, deprived of the solidity of an older identity. The carapace represents this identity which becomes stronger with time.

If you are about to change, if you are in the process of changing and you are feeling this type of emotion, it is completely normal. You just need to be patient and see the process through, and the only way to do this is to have compassion for yourself. Treat yourself with gentleness, tenderness and love. Be the teenager who changes because they are losing their shell and the protective parent who watches and helps them. These two people live together in you; listen to their messages.

...

"To live is to change – this is the lesson that the seasons teach us."

PAULO COELHO

...

When it comes time to change, you run the risk of nostalgia... The past holds a great fascination for people who are afraid of change or refuse to change for fear of its consequences. And nostalgia is like an intoxicating drink which stops you having to look to the future. If you start to feel this way, you're going in the wrong direction; you've taken a dead end. You need to go back and get back on the road to the future.

• • •

The past has its source in the future.

• • •

To avoid becoming nostalgic, you must try to turn change into an opportunity. You must have confidence in the future. You must have confidence in yourself – this is both a duty and proof of intelligence. Just as the caterpillar doesn't know that by becoming a butterfly it will be able to fly, someone who loses their job, gets divorced or goes bankrupt doesn't know that this major change will actually bring them great joy and open up new possibilities in their life.

Adolescents don't know that when they become adults, they will become beings with capacities, skills and rights that they currently lack. They think it better to remain an adolescent without responsibilities, who goes to school and has fun with his friends... But when he becomes an adult, he becomes the master of his life, able to travel the world, to make a thousand encounters, to earn the money necessary to achieve his dreams, to leave his routine and protected life in the past and live a human adventure.

• • •

There are two types of people on earth: sedentary and nomadic. Thousands of years ago, sedentary people made the choice to stop travelling and settle down to enjoy the comfort and abundance of agriculture, while nomads continued to travel, to discover the world, choosing a life punctuated by permanent changes. In modern societies, we are mostly born sedentary, but we can also choose to become nomads.

• • •

In my room the bed was here, the wardrobe there, and in between was the table,
until the day I had had enough – I'd move the bed here and the wardrobe here.

For a while I felt invigorated, but after a few days...boredom returned. I concluded that the source of my boredom was the table, or rather its immutably central position.

So, I pushed the table over there, and the bed in the middle. Unconventionally.

This second novelty gave me a new boost, and while it lasted, I accepted the non-conformist discomfort it caused – I could no longer sleep with my face to the wall, which had always been my favourite position.

But after a while, the novelty faded, and only the discomfort remained, so I pushed the bed here and the wardrobe in the middle.

This time the change was radical. Indeed, having the wardrobe in the middle of the room was more than just anti-conformism. It was avant-garde.

As time passed, however... Ah, that damned "passing of time"! In short, even the wardrobe in the middle of the room no longer appeared novel and unusual to me.

I had to make a break, take a fundamental decision. If, within the framework defined above, no real change was possible, I needed to leave this framework completely. As soon as non-conformism proved to be insufficient, as soon as the avant-garde failed to produce any results, I needed a revolution. So, I made the decision to sleep in the wardrobe. Anyone who has tried to sleep standing up in a wardrobe knows that it's so uncomfortable that sleep is impossible, not to mention exhausting for your legs and painful for your spine.

Yes, it was the right decision. Success, complete victory. For this time, even the "passing of time" had no impact. After some time, not only was I not used to the change, that is to say the change still felt like change, but I felt the change more and more acutely, because the pain increased as time passed.

Everything would have been fine, had it not been for my physical resistance, which turned out to be limited. One night, I couldn't stand it any longer, so I climbed out of the wardrobe and lay down on the bed. I slept for three days and three nights then pushed the wardrobe against the wall and the table in the middle, because the wardrobe in the middle was just in the way. Now the bed is here, as before, the wardrobe there, and in between there is the table. When I'm bored, I remember the time when I was a revolutionary[*].

• • •

"Be the change you wish to see in this world."

GANDHI

• • •

In your life, take the initiative for change. If you look ahead, you'll be the master of your life and avoid having to undergo unwanted changes. If this happens, accept them with humility

---

[*] This text is taken from the book: *Life is difficult* (1991).

without falling into despair. Don't feel sorry for yourself, take action until you take back control. Pay attention, because the opportunities are there, it's up to you to discover them and see them by looking at things with new eyes. Change the way you look at things and you'll see your life in a different way – then the change will be an extraordinary experience.

. . .

There are two types of people in life: the established and the outsiders. Established people have been working for a long time in a place, a sector or a profession. They know it all and their background gives them access to all every advantage. Outsiders are newcomers. They have no previous experience and for them life is much more difficult. When things change, the most difficult thing is to go from being an established person to being an outsider. The price of change is therefore often that of humility.

. . .

"Humility makes one invulnerable."

MARIE VON EBNER-ESCHENBACH

. . .

As you will have understood, change is always a test. It makes you face the powerlessness of seeing your situation change. The only countermeasure is the desire for change, life being change. The desire for change is nothing more than a desire to live. If you really desire to live your life, then every change will be welcomed as a blessing. Even if the changes bring difficult times, I'm convinced you'll make the most of them.

Being in conflict

WHEN I SAW YOU, YOU WERE IN CONFLICT...
IT WAS EXHAUSTING AND DAMAGING YOU PROFOUNDLY

HERE'S WHAT I'D HAVE LIKED TO TELL YOU... TO HELP YOU
RESOLVE THIS CONFLICT AND OVERCOME IT...

...I WOULD PROBABLY HAVE STARTED BY TELLING YOU
THIS STORY.

A long time ago, men and women who wanted to demonstrate their power had the idea of building a tower into the sky with the aim of reaching God. At that time, all the men and women on earth spoke only one language.

God, who did not approve of the construction of this tower, which he thought was a symbol of pride and arrogance, decided to prevent them from doing so. So, he made everyone building the tower speak in different languages.

The men and women who built the tower found it impossible to get along. Construction stopped and all the men and women scattered over the surface of the earth.

• • •

Conflicts are often caused by language. When the protagonists speak different languages, this creates misunderstandings, which generate frustrations that can turn into lasting conflict. The first thing to do to resolve a conflict is therefore to try to speak the other's language. This requires a special effort, because other people's language is difficult to speak, more difficult than a foreign language, because there is often no dictionary to facilitate learning.

Therefore, you must take the time to understand the meaning of the words your interlocutor is using. Pay attention to the intonations of your voice and the emotions that pass through your eyes. You need to ask questions to explain what they are thinking or feeling. A word might not have the same meaning for two people. It can be discovered, even after living next to someone for ten years. A better understanding of the other person helps us to identify the origins of the conflict and how to overcome it.

• • •

Once upon a time there were two tribes called the Pocoroh and the Pocorah, each of which lived on a mountain. The two tribes didn't like each other and regularly waged war. The first tribe would accuse the other of stealing water from the river, while the second tribe would accuse the other of stealing grass from the prairies. Whenever there was a disaster, the first tribe would accuse the second and the second would accuse the first. It was a vicious circle that led them to call each other names, throw insults and fight.

One day, a wise man passing by witnessed a fight that left many people injured. As he was a good man, he set about reconciling the two tribes, so he went to the Pocorohs and suggested to their chief that he make a trip. The chief was very reluctant, but the wise man finally convinced him. They went down the mountain and then climbed the other mountain. On the way back up, the chief of the Pocorohs discovered that the Pocorahs were able to grow maize and wheat.

That was why they drew water from the river.

They spent a few days on the mountain exploring and meeting its inhabitants. Then they set off again, and the wise man then asked the chief of the Pocorah to make a trip. He managed to convince him, blindfolded him and took him up the second mountain. On the way up, the chief of the Pocorahs discovered that the Pocorohs raised cows and sheep, so the Pocoroh could eat meat in abundance. Hay was used to feed them all year round, even in winter.

That was why they took the grass from the meadows.

Following this trip, the two tribes decided to exchange their knowledge of agriculture and animal husbandry. The Pocorah learned how to grow wheat and corn and the Pocoroh learned how to raise cows and sheep. The wise man went on his way, sure that there would be no more conflict between the two tribes. He had taught them to see what they could bring to each other. Rather than war, they could work together. Men are great when they work together! he thought to himself as he walked through the wilderness.

• • •

Conflict consumes a great deal of time and energy. It is destructive, so a compromise must be reached quickly. This compromise can only be built by listening to the needs of the other. If I listen to the needs of the other, then I can try to find a solution that will enable me, despite the disagreement, to find an answer to everyone's needs. It is therefore necessary to identify the needs of each person. This is what is called climbing each other's mountain.

• • •

*"Do not judge your neighbour until you have walked
for two moons in his moccasins."*

NATIVE AMERICAN PROVERB

• • •

One beautiful sunny morning, the Buddha was meditating in the presence of his disciples when a woman approached him.

"Does God exist?" she asked.
"Of course he exists," replied the Buddha.
After lunch, another woman approached.
"Does God exist?" she asked.
"Of course he doesn't exist," replied the Buddha.
"At the end of the afternoon", a third woman appeared to question the Buddha.
"Does God exist?" she asked.
"There is no single answer to this question. It's up to you to choose the answer that suits you," replied the Buddha.

After the woman had left, one of the disciples, who often became angry, exclaimed in revolt: "Master, I don't understand, this is absurd! Why do you give different answers to the same question?"
The Buddha smiled and gave him a compassionate look that immediately calmed the young man. Then he said: "Because they are different people, each one will come to the knowledge of God in his own way".
The first woman will take my word for it.
The second woman will do anything to prove me wrong.
The third woman will only believe what she decides herself.
This is what men and women are like, all different.

. . .

Sometimes conflict cannot be overcome because no compromise can be found. You can then ask for the intervention of a mediator to help you to find a compromise with your opponent. The mediator can come up with a solution that has not yet been devised – having no partisan interests, they can propose a balanced solution. It is an extra help in resolving a conflict. Never hesitate to call on a trusted third party to help you find a solution.

. . .

*"They make fun of children who justify their bad deeds
with this complaint: "He started it!"
But no adult conflict has its genesis elsewhere."*

AMÉLIE NOTHOMB

. . .

Conflicts never arise from a situation but always from a difference of viewpoint on a situation. A conflict often reveals profound differences in values. If you are reacting so strongly, it's because the other person "shocks" "your values" with their behaviour. In this way they affect you, sometimes unintentionally, in the depths of your heart, which is why a harmless act can provoke such a strong reaction. It's not the act that creates the reaction, but how the act affects you deep down in your being.

If you are in conflict with someone, ask yourself about the values that guide your life. You may find that the person's behaviour goes against your values. You can then thank them for helping you get to know yourself better. You can then decide to confront them, avoid them or accept them for who they are. You may also question your values and find out whether they are useful to you. Respecting your values means respecting yourself. But your values should never lead you to violence.

• • •

Once upon a time there was a young boy who was truly fortunate because he had been given every advantage from birth. And for good reason – he had been born into a rich and powerful family. He was also born with an IQ well above average and was very handsome. To top it all off, he was endowed with Herculean physical strength.

His parents were proud of their son and had great ambitions for him. They saw him as an extension of their own life and were willing to do anything to see him reach the highest positions.

They enrolled him in the best school with the best teachers. And as this was not enough, they also employed private tutors. When their son was fifteen, he excelled in every subject: literature, history, science and mathematics.

Apart from school and the time he spent studying, they made sure their son practised several sports. As he possessed extraordinary physical strength, it was not long before he excelled in each of them, winning all the competitions he took part in.

He also learned the arts: painting, sculpture, writing, in which he excelled equally well. For he was capable of great precision, while at the same time being extremely inventive when necessary.

To make him even more handsome, they had the most beautiful fabrics purchased and asked for beautiful clothes to be created for him. Thus dressed, the boy, who was already first in class and first in all sports disciplines, also became the most handsome boy in the universe.

When they had accomplished all this, the boy's parents imagined the greatest future for him: he was to become President, or head of a multinational company, or a top athlete, or a renowned artist, or all four at once.

To realise this vision, they went to an oracle who could predict predicting the future of young people. All he had to do was to observe them. Then he would close his eyes and receive visions that clearly indicated what the person's future would be.
The oracle had never been wrong about any prophecy.
He looked carefully at the young boy and was immediately struck by his beauty and charisma. Then he closed his eyes for a long time. His face tensed slightly and when he opened his eyes again, he said:
"This boy has all the assets to succeed, but he won't succeed."
His parents returned home terribly upset and decided to prove the oracle wrong, so they redoubled their efforts. Thanks to all the lessons and training, he became even more beautiful, even more intelligent, and even stronger than he already was.
Yet the oracle's prediction came to pass.
Their son had every quality, but he was hated.
His comrades, vexed by the fact that he was always the best at everything, spent their time plotting against him. They harassed him to the point of making him unhappy.
His teachers considered him self-righteous and were stingy with their knowledge. They didn't want to teach him.
In sports, nobody wanted him on their team. And in individual sports, nobody wanted him as an opponent.
In artistic activities, critics judged his work to be too far ahead of its time and nobody wanted to display it.

The young boy had received all but one quality from nature and his education. He had never learnt to be interested in others and to value them. But isn't this the basic need of every human being?

People felt ill at ease in his presence. They felt inferior and never had any space to shine or stand out. Or they felt humiliated and ran away from these situations.

The young boy, so handsome, so intelligent and so strong, soon found himself alone. No success is possible without being alone. He ended his life as a hermit, living in a remote part of the world and died without ever having accomplished anything great.

• • •

Conflict is a test. It is an opportunity to learn and develop one's inner self. Every conflict is an opportunity for you to better manage your inner states. Think of each conflict as a challenge and each challenge as a game. You must find the key to open the heart of your opponent, and if you find the key, then his heart will open, and he will become your best friend. This is a huge challenge for you.

• • •

"Difficulties should spur action, not discourage.
The spirit of man will be strengthened by conflict."

WILLIAM ELLERY CHANNING

• • •

There are three ways to resolve a conflict. Either you triumph by force but make a permanent enemy – the one you have fought and defeated will never stop wanting revenge. Or you'll triumph through Love. In this case, it is your ability to believe in the other that will allow you to solve the problem. Stop being a warrior and don the wise man's outfit and accept to forgive and love your opponent. By loving your opponent, you'll help him discover a new part of yourself.

• • •

"Wherever there is conflict, wherever you are confronted with an opponent, triumph over him with love."

GANDHI

• • •

Are you familiar with the four Toltec agreements*? They can help you to prevent conflicts. Here they are:

"Be impeccable with your word"

Always speak with integrity. Only say what you really think. Don't have thoughts or use words against yourself. Never use words to slander or criticise others. Speech should be used in the sense of truth and love. Speech is a tool that can build or destroy. Become aware of its power and master it. Never use lies or slander. Be true and build more authentic and harmonious relationships.

"Don't take anything personally"

You are never the cause of other people's actions. What others say and do is merely the result of their desires, needs, emotions and fantasies. The day you realise that you are not the cause or origin of other people's actions, you are set free. The father is not responsible for the son's actions, the daughter is not responsible for the mother's actions, the leader is not responsible for the subordinate's actions etc. By becoming aware of this reality, you restore the other person's freedom and responsibility.

"Don't make assumptions"

_____

* The four Toltec agreements (2016).

When you are stressed or anxious, you imagine the worst. Nothing is worse, because by constantly making negative assumptions, you end up believing them. You turn assumptions into certainties. When you imagine something, dare to ask questions, and express your needs to check whether what you think is true. Communicate clearly with others and avoid the sadness and anxiety that comes from misunderstandings and thoughts, actions or intentions that don't exist, but are just imagined.

"Always do your best"

You don't have to succeed in everything you do. The only obligation is to always do your best, which changes according to the context. Whatever the circumstances, do your best. Don't judge yourself, don't feel guilty, never have regrets, because the past can only be changed by acting and building your future. Try, try, fail. On the day you fail, be indulgent with yourself. You cannot be perfect and always victorious.

Goodbye

You're approaching the end and it's time to say goodbye. Thank you for taking the time to listen to me. Thank you so much for your precious time.

What else is there to add?

Life is a real challenge. There are conflicts, problems, difficulties, separations, failures, twists of fate, successes and failures...

All this requires great wisdom if one wishes to maintain one's inner well-being.

I think there are four principles that can help you make the world more comfortable and these events easier.

The first principle is love. You must feel love, but first for yourself. Love is different from being in love or passionate. Love is what you feel when you deeply and unconditionally want a living being to be able to grow and live well. To love is to want to see a person vibrate in their own way. If you feel love for yourself and for those around you, then you'll feel truly well and in harmony.

Can you love and embody the image of a virile male? Of course, you can; it's time for you to be just a human being and no longer conform to the harsh image that society is trying to impose on you.

The second principle is gratitude. To act is to give. But it's also necessary to learn to receive. Like when you breathe – when you breathe in, you receive oxygen from nature and this allows you to live, and when you breathe out you give carbon which will be used by plants to breathe. Learn to give and receive as you breathe. Act for others and accept the gifts of life and you'll soon see that everything will become more fluid, softer and easier for you and your loved ones.

The third principle is to trust life. It's good to have confidence in oneself, in one's physical and intellectual capacities, to overcome the obstacles and challenges of life. But it's even more useful to have confidence in life. Imagine that you're swimming in the middle of the sea. You can trust your hands and feet to keep you on the surface. But you can also trust the sea and its ability to carry you.

One day, when you're swimming in the sea, try this exercise – stop moving. Lie down fully. Let your head rest on the water and give up. You'll see that your body floats – the sea is carrying it as life carries you. If you trust life, then you can let go. You can let luck smile on you and activate the positive forces that are at work. You'll see many problems resolve themselves and you'll finally be able to breathe and let yourself go, joyfully.

• • •

*"The bird doesn't fly. It is the air that carries it.
The fish does not float. It is the water that carries it."*

CHINESE PROVERB

• • •

The fourth principle is the power of joy. The world you live in is a painting and you are the painter of this painting. It is you who decides every day what you want to depict in it. Your actions and thoughts are your brushes, and the colour represents your emotions. You can choose to paint a grey painting with frightening forms full of sadness every day, but you can also choose to paint picture painting with shimmering colours. This is the power of joy.

Never forget. It is not the outside world that determines your inner world. You have within you the power to transform your inner world and to transform your outer world. So, joy has the power to turn trials into opportunities, obstacles into opportunities to grow, sorrows into hopes... Joy was in you when you were a child. All you must do to regain it is to remember it. Let joy fill your whole being and you'll see the world and the people change before your eyes as if by a miracle.

I wish you all the best in this, because I always wish you well.

Goodbye and see you soon...

You liked this book. It was useful to you, so think very hard about someone you love: a friend, a family member, a colleague, the person you are in love with. Think about someone you love and who has recently been facing hardships. Give them a copy of this book. It will be a demonstration of love, interest and sensitivity. And who knows? Maybe they will like it and it will be useful. Then they will also want to gift it in turn, meaning the book will pass from hand to hand as a message of affection and benevolence. And together we will make the world a better place!

The Sound Of Silence
(The Sound of Silence)

Hello darkness, my old friend
I've come to talk with you again
Because a vision softly creeping
Left its seeds while I was sleeping
And the vision that was planted in my brain
Still remains
Within the sound of silence

In restless dreams I walked alone
Narrow streets of cobblestone
'Neath the halo of a streetlamp
I turned my collar to the cold and damp
When my eyes were stabbed by the flash of a neon light
That split the night
And touched the sound of silence

And in the naked light, I saw
Ten thousand people, maybe more
People talking without speaking
People hearing without listening
People writing songs that voices never share
And no one dared
Disturb the sound of silence

"Fools", said I, "You do not know
Silence like a cancer grows
Hear my words that I might teach you

Take my arms that I might reach you"
But my words, like silent raindrops fell
And echoed
In the wells of silence

And the people bowed and prayed
To the neon god they made
And the sign flashed out its warning
In the words that it was forming
And the sign said, "The words of the prophets are written on
the subway walls
And tenement halls"
And whispered in the sound of silence

SIMON & GARFUNKEL, 1964

THE ANSWER TO THE QUESTION ASKED AT THE BEGINNING OF THIS BOOK

At the beginning of this book, I asked you to name three animals that immediately come to mind

The first animal represents the way you see yourself.

The second animal represents how others perceive you.

The third is who you really are.

Bibliography

Butteau, P. (2002). *Manager, un véritable jeu avec la PNL*. Paris: Arnaud Franel Éditions.

Buzati, D. (1966). Le "K". Rome: Arnoldo Mondadori Editore.

Butterworth, E. (2000), *Discover the Power Within You by Butterworth*. Paperback.

Lebreton, E. (2017). *L'hypnose: la clé du bonheur*. Paris: Éditions Inpress.

Leroux, P. (2011). *Pour le cœur et pour l'esprit*. Québec: un monde différent.

Mrożek, S (1991). *La vie est difficile*. Paris: Albin Michel.

Rosenberg, M. (2004). *Les mots sont des fenêtres (ou bien ce sont des murs): Introduction à la*
Communication Non Violente. Paris: Editions de la découverte.

Ruiz, M. (2016). *Les quatre accords toltèques: La voie de la liberté personnelle*. Archamps: Éditions Jouvence.

By the same author

Lebreton, E. (2017). *L'hypnose: la clé du bonheur.* Paris: Éditions Inpress.

Lebreton, E. (2017). *10 attitudes gagnantes pour réussir dans la vie.* Paris: Éditions Maxima.

Goldman, M., & Lebreton, E. (2017). *50 histoires inspirantes pour être heureux.* Paris: Éditions Orient'Action®.

Lebreton, E. (2016). *La méthode 10/10: perdre dix kilos et vivre 10 ans de plus.* Paris: Éditions Orient'Action®.

One last story before you go...

Once upon a time there was a tribe living somewhere in Africa. In this tribe, a child's birthday was born was not the day it was born, nor the day it was conceived, but the day its mother had imagined in her dreams that it would come. In this tribe, when a woman decided to have a child, she would sit at the foot of a tree and listen until she could hear the song of the child that wanted to be born. When she had heard the song of that child, she would return to the village to see the man who would be her father. She would then teach him the child's song, and when they made love, they would both sing the child's song as an invitation.

When the mother was pregnant, she taught the child's song to the midwives and other elderly women in the village. When the child was born, the midwife and the elderly women of the village would sing her song to the child in welcome. When the child grew up, the other villagers would learn his song. If the child fell or was hurt, the person who saw the child was sad could sing the song to comfort the child. If the child did something wonderful or went through puberty rites, then the members of the tribe would sing his song. And the child would feel honoured and proud because he was recognised by all members of the tribe.

In the tribe, there was another important moment when the inhabitants of the village would sing the song. If in his life the person committed a crime or wrongdoing, he was called to the centre of the village, and all the inhabitants would then form a circle around him. Then they would sing his song. The tribe was aware that bad behaviour was not corrected by punishment, but by love and the reminder of identity. When a person recognises their song, they no longer need to do wrong, because they know who they are and where they come from. And that is how members of the community who broke the rules were invited to get back on the right path.

All his life, the person could recognise himself and be recognised through his song... When he got married, when his birthday came, when he did something good for others... And when the day of his death came, all the villagers gathered around the deceased's bed could change his song, one last time, to accompany him to the afterlife. And this song made this final ordeal sweeter. And later, when the living wanted to remember the person they had loved and lost, then they could sing his song and feel his presence. It was a way to keep the person alive long after death.

You didn't grow up in that tribe in Africa that sings your song during crucial moments in life. Yet you too have a song, and life reminds you of it. When you are in harmony with yourself, when you feel good, it means that your life, your actions, your experiences, your emotions are consistent with your song. And when you feel bad, it means that your life, your actions, your experiences, your emotions are no longer consistent with your song. You can also find out what your song is and sing it. Try to find your song, let it come like a whisper with the thoughts that accompany it because it is what you are deep inside yourself.

Remember your song...

TRAINING PROGRAMME PERSONAL AND PROFESSIONAL COACHING

1 PRESENTATION OF THE "coaching" ACTIVITY

We know of no more powerful tool for professional (and personal) development than coaching. People who benefit from this type of coaching make lasting changes. They have more self-confidence, they are more assertive, but also more efficient and effective in their work. They are also more serene and more balanced, even when they are called upon to assume great responsibilities within the organisation. Coaching is a strategy to become happier and more efficient in their work and life. Coaching consists of:

- Changing the way you see a situation, enriching it and developing it to give you more effective strategies for reading situations,
- Knowing how to use all your intellectual, emotional and relational resources to find a solution to professional or personal problems.

Coaching is now a service used regularly by companies and is marketed as a programme in individual or group format. Costs vary from 80 euro/hour for individually funded personal coaching to 250 euro/hour for professional coaching programmes for executives or senior managers.

2 OBJECTIVE OF THE "COACHING" TRAINING COURSE

At the end of the course, you'll be able to support a person in personal or professional coaching.

3 DURATION OF THE "COACHING" TRAINING COURSE

40 hours of training in total, including:

- 40 hours, i.e. 5 days of face-to-face training,
- *Assistance by telephone/email for your first coaching.*

4 EDUCATIONAL CONTENT OF THE "COACHING" TRAINING COURSE

The coaching course offered by Orient'Action® covers the essential themes to acquire the fundamental skills of the coaching profession. Developed by a doctor in psychology, researcher and practitioner, the Orient'Action® coaching method is at once scientific, pragmatic and operational and based on the main principles of positive psychology. It gives access to innovative techniques in the field of coaching, making it a benchmark.

1. The approach of the personal and professional coach:

- How to position oneself in the relationship with the student?
- The difference between counsellor, consultant, psychologist and coach,
- Specific coaching situations: co-development, coaching in companies,
- Ethics and deontology of the coach.

2. Step 1: Diagnosis of the situation

- Analysing and assessing the underlying need for coaching,
- Apprehending and analysing the situation, transferring the tools to the student so that he or she can take the lead and enrich his or her understanding,
- Identifying and updating the obstacles preventing the transformations needed to progress, solve the problem, overcome the obstacle or meet the challenge.

3. Support techniques

To be successful in coaching, knowledge of the human being and coaching techniques are essential. Here are the seven techniques we use in the Orient'Action® coaching method.

- **Technique no. 1:** tools for self-knowledge and carrying out the diagnosis,
- **Technique no. 2:** "take a seat" and "choose",
- **Technique no. 3:** projective techniques,
- **Technique no. 4:** neurolinguistic programming and hypnosis,
- **Technique no. 5:** commitment,

- **Technique no. 6:** speaking the language of the unconscious,
- **Technique no. 7:** Rituals.

Each technique is approached from two angles: theoretical and operational. Through numerous practical exercises, you are led to put yourself in a situation where you can use and apply a given technique. You'll thus acquire a solid capacity to provide support.

⑤ CERTIFICATE AWARDED AT THE END OF THE "COACHING" COURSE

This course leads to a certificate of competence in personal and professional coaching, which certificate gives access to all the tools and methodological media used by Orient'Action® in the context of coaching. The awarding of this diploma is conditional upon the successful completion of an evaluation test consisting of a multiple-choice questionnaire and a written report on an individual coaching case.

⑥ COST OF THE COACHING COURSE

To find out our rates, contact us on info@orientacton.com.

THE FRENCH METHOD

Emeric Lebreton
Doctor in psychology

THE FRENCH METHOD
LOSE WEIGHT AND LIVE LONGER

Check this out